M. I. STEBLIN-
KAMENSKIJ

The Saga Mind

Translated by

KENNETH H. OBER

ODENSE UNIVERSITY PRESS 1973

ISBN 87 7492 069 3
Andelsbogtrykkeriet i Odense

Contents

An editorial preface

The book *Mir sagi*, which Professor M. I. Steblin-Kamenskij of Leningrad published in 1971, was promptly translated, for fun, by Mr Kenneth Ober, now of the University of Illinois. His English version subsequently had the benefit of a reading by Professor Steblin-Kamenskij. Dr E. L. Bredsdorff, Reader in Scandinavian Studies and Fellow of Peterhouse, Cambridge, brought the translation to my notice, and I happily read it. I then recommended it to Mr Hans Bekker-Nielsen, Reader in Norse Philology, Odense University, and to Mr Torkil Olsen, whose enterprise as Librarian of Odense University is matched, as far as I can see, only by his enterprise as Managing Director of Odense University Press. Publication has followed, eased by a modest financial guarantee from the Council of the Viking Society for Northern Research in London. In acting as a kind of General Editor I have been lucky enough to have the aid and advice of my brother, Mr Paul Foote, University Lecturer in Russian and Fellow of The Queen's College, Oxford. It may be noted that no modification of the bibliographical information given at the end of the book has been made; it offers, among other things, a welcome introduction to saga-scholarship in the U.S.S.R.

In this model instance of international and inter-university co-operation it is hard to know who should be grateful to whom, but I am sure that all who are interested in Old Icelandic literature will appreciate every effort that has gone into making the book available in English. For Professor Steblin-Kamenskij makes us re-think our premises and persuades us to this hard and healthy exercise by his fresh insights, an engaging, sardonic manner, and many demonstrations of argumentative skill. His book must lead to lively and profitable debate; and our answers to questions like "What is a saga, and why?" will never be quite the same again.

Peter Foote
Department of Scandinavian Studies,
University College London

Foreword

> But whatever is incorrectly stated in these writings must yield to that which proves more truthful.
>
> *Ari inn fróði*

This book is about the spiritual world of the family sagas – the most remarkable works of Icelandic literature and the most original literary monuments of medieval Europe. A great deal has been written concerning these sagas, and they have been investigated in detail from many points of view. But their spiritual world – their conceptions of truth, human personality, form and content, good and evil, time and space, life and death – has attracted little scholarly attention. The author ventures to repeat what he wrote in the foreword to his *Kul'tura Islandii*, which appeared in 1967:

> A popular form of exposition has been adopted in this book, not because it imparts the right to by-pass difficult problems or to oversimplify them, but on the contrary, because it permits concentration on the essence of the problems examined and does not encumber the exposition with retelling the works of others, with enumerating names, dates and facts, with references, with footnotes, and the other ballast inevitable in any work intended for scholarly specialists.

Judging by the numerous and favorable comments, for which the author is very grateful, that book struck a responsive chord in the reader. Therefore, summing up his saga investigations in the area of the history of the human mind, the author again prefers to address a wide circle of readers and not only scholarly specialists.

A bibliography of the family sagas and some information about them are to be found in the comments and notes at the end of the book.

Is there a point to literary history?

> The past is of cultural interest only when it is still the present or may yet become the future.
>
> *Edward Sapir*

It is a well-known fact that artistic monuments of remote periods can arouse the admiration of a modern man. Millions of people in our own time admire the architectural monuments of antiquity, the arches and stained glass windows of Gothic cathedrals, and the old Russian icons and frescoes. And although with the help of modern technology it is possible to imitate any of the ancient artistic monuments, nonetheless our admiration is aroused only by the monuments themselves and not by their imitations (if, of course, we are qualified to distinguish the original from the imitation). Why can the artistic monuments of remote ages arouse our admiration? In a very general way, it is not difficult to answer this question. A modern man can feel the artistic uniqueness of these monuments; he feels in them esthetic values which at one time could be created spontaneously, but which in our time can only be imitated. Is it not possible in such a case to determine what comprises the artistic uniqueness of each monument of the remote past? Yes, this is probably possible, and it ought undoubtedly to be the main preoccupation of the art experts.

Admittedly, they usually prefer to give us as much information as possible on each individual monument – its dimensions, material, history, and the like – i.e., they describe it in as much detail as possible. It is as if they recognize that in fact the artistic uniqueness of a monument is most apparent from immediate contemplation of it, and they naively assume that sufficiently detailed information or a sufficiently precise description can give us an adequate substitute for this immediate contemplation. In any case, it seems that whoever is capable of feeling the artistic uniqueness of a monument of the remote past does not, as a rule, seek its definition in the works of art experts. Artistic monuments are accessible to our sense organs – it is after all monuments of architecture, sculpture or painting we speak of, not literary works. And can the words of an art expert compete with our sense organs? For this same reason, if an art expert describes not the monuments themselves but the impression which, in his view, they should produce on us (" ... makes a great impression", "amazingly beatiful", "exceptionally fine", and the like), such descriptions can by no means replace for us our own immediate impressions.

It is a completely different matter with literary monuments of the remote past. A literary work does not act immediately on our sense organs. It is not a visible and tangible object. It is a spiritual entity. And we apprehend this spiritual entity through signs or symbols of something in our consciousness – symbols apprehended moreover in their symbolic reflection, symbols of symbols. These symbols are words, and the symbols of symbols are written words.

Admittedly, even when a work of art is a visible and tangible object, it is not simply an object existing by itself, independent of the person perceiving it, but it is an object perceived in a definite manner, created for such perception, and not existing outside it. In other words, such a work of art is always both a material and a spiritual entity. But a literary work is something purely spiritual. It is not an expression of the spiritual world through a visible and tangible exterior. It is therefore natural that literature of remote ages should be inseparable from the spiritual world of the people among whom it originated, and cannot be understood by modern man if he does not understand this spiritual world.

In attempting to make an ancient literary monument comprehensible to modern man, literary historians sometimes compare it to a given work of architecture or pictorial art of the same period – a Gothic cathedral, old frescoes, and the like. In this way the immediacy characteristic of the impression made by visible and tangible works of art is attributed to the impression made by the literary work. But this is the whole point – in contrast to literary works, visible and tangible works of art express a spiritual world not through symbols of symbols, but through material substances. So the comparison of ancient literary works with works of other arts is essentially only an attempt to produce a sort of optical illusion.

A dual barrier separates modern man from ancient literature: the symbols through which it is expressed, words; and the symbols of these symbols, the written reflections of words.

Words are a barrier because these are words of an ancient language, suited to the expression of something in the consciousness of a person living in a remote age, a consciousness completely dissimilar to ours. The meanings of words of an ancient language always differ to a greater or lesser degree from the meanings of corresponding words in a modern language. And they invariably differ most of all where the divergence is most difficult to note – in the most elementary words concerning the spiritual world, such as "soul", "truth", "good", and so on. Even the man who reads an ancient work in the original actually reads it in translation – inevitably he inserts, to some degree, his own accustomed meanings into the words of the ancient language, and thus, so to speak, translates the words of the ancient language into a modern language. But by the same token, the person who reads an ancient work only in translation and not in the original, is actually reading it in a translation of a translation.[1]

The written reflections of words also constitute a barrier because the investigator naturally gets the idea that the goal of the investigation lies in these reflections themselves. He is engrossed by the manuscripts, the material monuments in which the old literature is represented rather than by the literary works encoded in these material monuments or the spiritual world expressed in these works. The goal of the investigation becomes the decoding of the material monument – its decipherment, the establishment of peculiarities of script, paleography and orthography, the determining of time and place of writing. Thus, ancient manuscripts or copies of them are material monuments of a quite special type – not only do they not make the works presented in them immediately accessible to our sense organs, they do just the opposite – they obscure them from the investigator. Indeed, in order to investigate these material monuments, it is essential to concentrate on them as something *per se*, and so reject immediate perception of the literature presented in them.

In fact, such a rejection usually takes place not only in the investigation of manuscripts themselves but also in any purely philological investigation to do with the composition, text, sources, or provenience of a given work, and in the description of everything which has already been written about it. It goes without saying that all such investigations are both inevitable and necessary. Nevertheless, this does not preclude the fact that the investigator of an ancient piece of literature often apprehends no more of the work itself and of the spiritual world expressed in it than a worm gnawing the parchment on which it is set forth. A research worker may, of course, perfectly understand his thankless role and possess a sense of humor, something hardly possible in the case of the worm. Admittedly, it may also be absent in the case of the research worker.

A philological study of old literary monuments implies, so to speak, a fundamental rejection of the distinction between the more important and the less important. If the works are important, then any information concerning the manuscripts containing these works is also important, and so, for instance, is any information concerning the man thanks to whom these manuscripts were preserved. Consequently, any information about his wife, her origin, and her way of life is also important. And if it is known that she was previously married to someone else, then any information about her first husband is also important – for instance, a detailed description of any documents which could serve as material for his biography, or at least for the biography of someone among his possible kinsmen. (Here the author has permitted himself to summarize the contents of a certain philological investigation which appeared recently.[2])

But even if in a philological study of an ancient literary monument there is a place for esthetic evaluations – for the apprehension of this monument as an artistic work – their role, in comparison with the role such evaluations play in studies of modern literature, is as a rule negligible: they prove to be merely pendants, alien to the general aim of the work. In fact, until recently, the study of literatures of the distant past, for instance medieval literature, was not literary history in the true sense of the word. Relative to modern literature – where literature has not yet become history – the historical point of view has been dominant, while relative to medieval literature – where literature has long since become history – the philological point of view, rather than the historical, has been dominant, i.e., the literary nature of the works and the spiritual world expressed in them have been virtually ignored.

Ignoring the spiritual world is also possible when an ancient literary monument is analyzed as an artistic work. It is possible, for example, to describe the separate elements of artistic form – prosody, style, and composition – without interest in them as an expression of the mind of the man of that time, but only in their possible presentation in statistical tables or symmetrical schemes, or "structures" (a word the popularity of which in modern linguistics – and recently also in literary criticism – is in inverse ratio to its actual content), and to think naively that the neatness of the tables and the symmetry of the schemes, or "structures", constitute the "art" which one should detect in the literary work. But in fact, schemes and tables hardly contribute more to the understanding of a literary work than a chemical analysis does to the understanding of a painting or piece of sculpture. But after all, chemists do not undertake to interpret works of art.[3]

There is yet another way of ignoring the spiritual world expressed in pieces of ancient literature. This is by ascribing a certain quality to a work – a quality of undefined content, a timeless quality, one not characteristic of any definite period. Such a quality may be given the name of "popular origin" for example. As a result of the extremely indefinite and timeless nature of such a quality, it can be freely attributed to any ancient literary work. Moreover, it is accepted as proven that the presence of this quality is a sign of the artistic excellence of a work. In this way, artistic excellence can be ascribed to any piece of ancient literature, while the spiritual world expressed in it can remain utterly ignored.

But in fact the commonest way to ignore the spiritual world expressed in ancient literary works is by what is called their "modernization". It is assumed they were intended to satisfy the same esthetic criteria and tastes as prevail in our time, and the same artistic merits are detected in them as modern man attributes to contemporary works.

On the other hand, it is generally quite difficult to prove that this form of ignoring the spiritual world of an ancient monument actually takes place. It is difficult for instance to refute the assertion that the essence of esthetic conceptions and criteria has remained the same in all times, and that consequently the modernization of ancient literary monuments is in principle impossible. It is assumed, in the terminology of cybernetics, that a literary work is a certain piece of "information", enciphered by means of a certain "code". One can, then, no more modernize an ancient literary work than decipher "information" without using the same "code" as it was enciphered in.

But if one considers the historical point of view obligatory not only in relation to human society but also in relation to the human spiritual world, then it is natural to assume that esthetic criteria and conceptions cannot have been identical at all times. A literary work then proves to be something much more complex than "information" enciphered by means of a certain "code". And in fact a literary work may evidently be apprehended and understood in different ways, and this is especially apparent in the case of the interpretation of a given work in different ages. In other words, a literary work can be different sorts of "information" depending on the "code" attributed to it. It is precisely this which makes possible the application of modern esthetic criteria to ancient literature, reading into it things which the people of its time could not see in it – in other words, its modernization. But such a treatment of ancient literature obviously means to a greater or lesser degree ignoring the spiritual world expressed in it and a kind of falsification, a transformation of it into something which shines, so to speak, with reflected light.

Moreover, to acknowledge that the modernizing of ancient literary works is possible, actually means acknowledging also that this modernizing is in some degree inevitable. Indeed, a modern man, unless he avoids esthetic evaluations altogether – which, as was said, often happens in philological investigations – cannot help applying the esthetic criteria prevalent in his own time. He is forced to do so first of all by the language he speaks. He cannot help applying to ancient literary monuments those concepts which are expressed in modern European languages by such terms as "belles-lettres", "realism", "author's contribution", "idea content", and so on, even though in the age when these monuments were created such words and such concepts did not exist. In attempting to understand the intent of an ancient author, the modern investigator resorts to accustomed modern words and concepts, and thereby ascribes to the author something of which he could not have conceived. Actually, the author may not have had the slightest idea that his work was "belles-lettres" – or even that he was an "author".

Modernizing suggests itself, for example, wherever an obvious external similarity to modern literary art is present in ancient literary works – it is natural to attribute to these works an internal similarity as well. The wide application of modern esthetic evaluations to the Old Icelandic family sagas which has taken place recently is, of course, due to the fact that it is not difficult to detect in these works a certain external similarity to the most widespread of modern genres, that of the realistic novel. As a result of this external similarity, it has been possible to read into the family sagas, to a certain extent, the internal world of us modern men – modern conceptions of artistic invention, and in part modern psychology, as when for example a sense of guilt in the spirit of Kafka is found in *Njáls saga*.

On the other hand, such a genre as skaldic poetry is as a rule completely unacceptable to a modern man. This poetry is too unlike modern poetry. In it there is not even external similarity to the poetry to which people of today are accustomed. For this reason, literary historians usually dismiss the artistic essence of skaldic verses with such brief remarks as "There is no poetry in these verses" – meaning of course "poetry" in our modern sense (which is, incidentally, completely different from the sense of the corresponding Old Icelandic word). An attempt at modernizing skaldic poetry, by interpreting it for example as formalistic experimentation analogical to the experimentation of modern poets, could hardly succeed – it would imply ignoring too obviously the essence of skaldic poetry – it would be too crude a modernizing attempt. In fact, refusal to acknowledge this poetry as poetry is also to modernize it, but only, as it were, with a minus sign. In its own time, skaldic poetry was thought of not only as real poetry, but as the only poetry possible. The refusal to acknowledge skaldic poetry as poetry means applying modern esthetic criteria to it, and ignoring the criteria it was created to satisfy, and this in turn means modernizing it.

Thus it is impossible for a modern man to cease being a modern man, impossible for him to renounce his ingrained conceptions and so renounce some modernizing of old literary works. But this modernizing can be neutralized – a modern man can come to understand how his conceptions differ from those of a man of another age, and thus also to understand the uniqueness of a work in which these conceptions are expressed. The application of our modern criteria to this work, which is to a certain degree inevitable, will then become a means of realizing its uniqueness. In other words, in order to overcome the inevitable modernizing of ancient pieces of literature, it is necessary to strive to understand the specific characteristics of the conceptions expressed in them.

But even if the pieces of ancient literature are understood in their uniqueness, will they not always satisfy modern man less than works created especially for his satisfaction, i.e., will they not essentially be only of historical interest? After all, old literary works were created to satisfy tastes completely different from ours, and in the process of literary development a certain progress had to take place – new, formerly unknown means of esthetic effect had to be worked out and then made general property. But this may be answered by the following: historical development in literature, as well as in art and in spiritual life in general, inevitably involves not only gains but also losses. For instance, progress in the means of expression in literature may be accompanied by regression in its content. Spiritual values which have been lost by the human race in its development may be forever preserved in ancient works of literature. If this is not so, is there any point to the history of literature? But only concrete investigations of ancient works of literature from the point of view of the conceptions presented in them can prove that this is indeed so.

What is truth?

> Where is the wisdom we have lost in knowledge?
> Where is the knowledge we have lost in information?
> *T. S. Eliot*

In scholarship it often happens that a concept, basic for a given important question, is taken for granted, as something that goes without saying, although in fact the solution of the given important question depends precisely on how this basic concept is understood. Is what is told in the family sagas true? What is the relation of truth and fiction in them? Exactly what in each of them is truth and what is fiction? These are the questions which have always been the most important ones asked about the family sagas. All else that remains questionable in relation to these works is closely bound up with these questions – their origin, the stages of their development, their sources or prototypes, their dating. But just what is the truth, about which so much is written in the literature concerning the family sagas? And can one speak of truth in these sagas without analyzing what truth is, in general?[4]

When one asserts this or that about "truth" in the family sagas, one of course has in mind – although this is never specified – our modern conceptions of what constitutes truth. But in fact do not these conceptions differ from those which prevailed in the society in which these sagas originated? If this is so, then everything that up to now has been stated about truth and fiction in the family sagas really brings us no closer to an understanding of whether they are truth or fiction than a color-blind man's assertion about a given color brings us to an understanding of what the color is.

Modern man's conceptions of truth, as well as many other areas of his consciousness, are characterized by duality, division, absence of unity. He recognizes two forms of truth. One finds its most complete expression in scholarly study for instance in the study of the past of human society – history. Only this study will be discussed here, since the division into two truths is most clearly expressed in what is told of the past.

"Historical truth" – we will so designate the truth presented in the study of history – is the exact report of what has occurred. The author believes that his report concerning the past is exact, or at least he wants others to believe this. But the diversity of individual facts of the past is inexhaustible. It is possible to establish exactly only certain individual facts of the past – its skeleton, so to speak – merely those which have significance for an entire given society, but by no means all the individual facts of the past, or all that has happened to individual persons in their private lives. The reality of the past in all its living fullness cannot be the content of an exact report representing historical truth. In all its living fullness, the reality of the past can only be synthesized or reproduced as the result of creative generalization. That means it can be the content of a work whose purpose is to evoke a vivid and living idea of the reality of the past, but not to report exact information about it. But such a generalization of single facts of the past is no longer truth in the proper sense of the word; it is "artistic truth", which is fiction. Whoever creates artistic truth is conscious that it is a creative reproduction of what might have been and not at all an exact report of what in reality was – in other words, he is conscious that it is not truth in the proper sense of the word. Those for whom the artistic truth is created are also conscious of this. But if artistic truth is taken for truth in the proper sense of the word – as happens with children, for example – this in modern civilization is a vestigial manifestation, a relic of the state of consciousness prevailing before there was a division into two truths.

Thus, of the modern man's two possible truths concerning the past, one is truth in the proper sense of the word, but not art; the other is art, but actually untruth. In other words, for the modern man, on the one hand, a truth concerning the past is possible which, as he himself knows, is really an untruth; and on the other hand, for him art and truth in the proper sense of the word are incompatible.

These two truths do not only imply, evoke, and limit each other, they are also in opposition to each other. A sharp and distinct boundary lies between them. Anything intermediate between them is impossible, just as anything is impossible halfway between what happened in reality and what did not happen in reality, but only might have happened. A novel telling of real events, or of people who really existed, is just as much a novel as any other. Even if there is truth in the proper sense of the word in it (facts taken from life, for example), they merely form the skeleton of the work, while its flesh and blood are made up of the reality reproduced through artistic creativity, i.e. artistic truth rather than truth in the proper sense of the word. The same author may, of course, write both a piece of scholarly research and a novel. But a historical investigation cannot be at the same time a novel, just as a historical novel is always a novel and not a scholarly investigation.

In the literature concerning the sagas it is, as a rule, tacitly assumed that the two forms of truth about the past that are characteristic of the consciousness of modern man also existed in the consciousness of the people in early Icelandic society. In accordance with this, the narrative material in the sagas is interpreted in one of three ways. It may be interpreted as historical truth. Then it is analyzed by methods of modern historical study – chronologies are checked and a comparison with evidence from other sources is carried out. Or the narrative material in the sagas is interpreted as artistic truth. Then it is analyzed like modern belletristic literature – it is taken wholly as the realization of the conceptual and artistic intentions of the author. Or – and this is most frequent – the narrative material is interpreted as something halfway between historical and artistic truth – something as impossible as a cross between a camel and a tiger – and then methods fundamentally contradicting one another are simultaneously applied in varying proportions. All ideas about the development of Old Icelandic literature, all classifications of the sagas, and all evaluations of the essence of each of them are the result of assigning them to one of the two rubrics to which modern man is accustomed, corresponding to the two forms of truth described above.

But did these two forms of truth exist in the consciousness of people in early Icelandic society? Very many facts indicate that only one form of truth existed for them – one which may be called "syncretic truth". Whoever reported syncretic truth about the past strove simultaneously for accuracy and for reproduction of reality in all its living fullness. But then this was not only truth in the proper sense of the word but also art, or an organic combination of what in the consciousness of modern man is incapable of combination. Syncretic truth is something lost for ever. It is by no means something in between the two other truths. It is far richer and has far greater content than both modern truths. It is fundamentally distinct from both of them. It is a third entity. For this reason, attempting to determine what in the sagas is historical truth and what is artistic truth is tantamount to seeking a difference whose very absence constitutes the essence of the truth presented in the sagas.

The fact that only one form of truth existed in the consciousness of people living in early Icelandic society is primarily attested by linguistic data.[5]

Such concepts as "historical truth", "artistic truth", and "artistic invention" or "fiction", which may be easily expressed in any modern language, including Modern Icelandic, find no expression at all in Old Icelandic, and consequently did not exist for the people of that time. In Old Icelandic there were only words and expressions which were closest in meaning to the modern "truth" and "lie". These words obviously had however a wider range of meaning than the corresponding words in modern European languages, since they could also refer to what one would call, from the modern point of view, "artistic truth" or "artistic invention", but never simply "truth" or "lie".

One might surmise that concepts such as "artistic truth" and "artistic invention" are most nearly equalled by what is described in Old Icelandic literature as "entertaining" though "lying". "This saga was told to King Sverrir, and he said that such lying sagas (*lygisǫgur*) were most entertaining (*skemmtiligastar*)" occurs in the well-known story of the feast at Reykjahólar. And in the story of the bull Brandkrossi there is the following passage: "Although this story seems doubtful to some, it is entertaining to listen to (*er gaman at heyra hana*)". In both cases it is a question of works whose truthfulness apparently aroused doubts because of their obvious lack of verisimilitude. On the other hand, in the bishops' sagas – works which beyond doubt were not considered "lying" and which from the modern point of view are certainly not "artistic" – it is stated several times that they are told "for entertainment" (*til gamans*) or that they are "fine entertainment" (*góð skemmtan*). Thus Old Icelandic words which we translate as "entertaining" obviously have nothing in common with the modern word "artistic".

There were also no words in Old Icelandic to denote works claiming to be only historical truth or only artistic truth. There was nothing analogical to such modern designations as "novel", "novella", "short story" or "drama", on the one hand, or "article", "investigation", "monograph", or dissertation" on the other. Consequently, the corresponding concepts were also non-existent. Therefore to assert, for example, that "the author of this saga wanted to write a novel, not a historical monograph" – and such assertions are frequently found in modern works on the family sagas – is just as absurd as attributing to the saga-writer an understanding of what a film scenario or a television show is.

In Old Icelandic there existed the universal word *saga* (apparently from *segja*, "to say, tell"), which denoted any narrative, written or oral. Its original meaning was probably "that which is said, narrated". This word could also designate the narrated events themselves: for example, "He was already very old at the time when these events (*sjá saga*) took place." And since the events told of in the saga were most often feuds, *saga* could also mean "feud". For example, "Thus originated the feud between Þorbjǫrn and Hávarðr the Lame (*saga þeira Þorbjarnar ok Hávarðar ins halta*)." But while in Modern Icelandic this word has two clearly distinct meanings – a saga as a literary work and history as a scholarly discipline – in Old Icelandic there is not the slightest trace of such a distinction. Whether a narrative was considered fact or fiction, it was designated by this word.

The same lack of distinction between the two truths,

the historical and the artistic, is understood in other, less frequently used Old Icelandic terms for narrative – *frásǫgn*, *frásaga* – as well as in the usual term for a more or less independent part of a narative – *þáttr*, literally "strand (of a rope)". It is frequently assumed that only historical truth is implied by the word *fræði* ("knowledge", "wisdom"). In Modern Icelandic this word has indeed acquired the meaning "scholarship", "learning". In Old Icelandic, however, it obviously denoted any knowledge, for instance knowledge of sagas, both oral and written, and it could also mean "writings", "incantations", and "verse". The meaning "scholarly learning" has been read into this word because in the *First Grammatical Treatise* it is applied to the writings of Ari inn fróði ("those bits of learning [*fræði*] which Ari Þorgilsson wrote down in books with great wisdom"), and Ari's writings are, comparatively, least dissimilar to what in our day is called "science" or "scholarship". The fact of the matter is that this "scholarship" of Ari's is an individual characteristic of his and not by any means the characteristic of a scholarly genre supposedly in existence at that time (cf. below, p. 44). Therefore the application of the word *fræði* to what was written down by Ari inn fróði is only a particular instance of the use of this word in its usual meaning of "knowledge".

Old Icelandic translated narratives, both historical and non-historical, were also designated by the word *saga*. In translated works there also sometimes occur the designations of literary works that were characteristic of medieval European literature – *dœmisaga* ("parable", literally "example-saga"), *æfisaga* or *lífssaga* ("biography", literally "life-saga"), and the like. But these designations all include, as a rule, the same word – *saga* – and were consequently thought of only as variants of what this word denoted.

These linguistic data attest unambiguously to the unity of truth in the consciousness of people in early Icelandic society. This indivisibility of truth also applied, of course, to the most original part of Old Icelandic prose literature, the family sagas, which also seem most original to people today, apparently just because the indivisibility of truth finds its fullest expression in them.

What did these works represent to those who created them, and to those for whom they were created? In the literature on the family sagas, it is customary either to by-pass this question completely or to give an evasive answer to it, while in fact only an exhaustive answer would permit an understanding of what constitutes the uniqueness of these works. In recent literature on the family sagas, it seems that the idea predominates – admittedly, usually only expressed indirectly – that they were considered fiction, created from given materials in precisely the same way as modern authors create their works, such as novels and short stories. In fact, from our modern point of view, the family sagas actually constitute – to a greater or lesser degree – artistic invention; and to the extent that they are seemingly true, they constitute artistic truth. But were they artistic invention or artistic truth from the point of view of the people in ancient Iceland? Obviously, neither. After all, such concepts did not exist.

When the intention of the author of one of the family sagas is said to have been artistic truth rather than historical truth, it is actually being asserted that his intention was to write a historical novel – a work which, though containing a sort of skeleton of historical facts, is basically fiction. Indeed, it is sometimes flatly asserted that the family sagas are historical novels by the intent of their authors. It is quite beyond doubt, of course, that the family sagas had certain literary prototypes. But could these prototypes be works that appeared six hundred years later? The historical novel, as is known, appeared as a genre only at the beginning of the nineteenth century (and in

Iceland not before the end of the century), and was the result of a lengthy process, the stages of which are well known. It may, of course, be assumed – and this too is sometimes done – that the prototype of a given saga was another saga, and this latter saga was actually a historical novel. But what was the prototype of this other saga? *Ivanhoe* or some other novel by Walter Scott? For the Icelanders of the thirteenth century, the family sagas were of course simply sagas (the family sagas have been thought of as a separate genre only in modern times – this will be discussed below), i.e. works in which the indivisibility of truth is implicit, and their prototypes could naturally have only been works of the same type.

More logical than considering the historical novel as the prototype of the family sagas would be to assume that their prototype was the courtly romance of Tristan and Isolde, a work originating in the twelfth century in France and first translated in Norway in 1226. Such an assumption has been made. Admittedly, it has been established that the first family sagas were written before 1226. But the chronological discrepancy is in this case not so great: at any rate, it is not six hundred years, as it would be if the family sagas were regarded as historical novels. Much worse is the fact that this assumption is based only on a misunderstanding of literary terms. The fact is that in most European languages both the medieval courtly romance and the modern realistic novel are designated by the same term (*roman*). These two genres characterize, respectively, two periods separated by half a millennium of intensive literary development, and they are as far removed from each other as the sky from the earth. In English these two genres are designated by different words ("romance" and "novel"), and if this were so in other languages, it would never have occurred to anyone to compare the family sagas with the courtly romance of

Tristan and Isolde, for while the sagas have something in common with the realistic novel, they have nothing at all with the courtly romance. In fact, the assumption that the prototype for the family sagas was the romance of Tristan and Isolde is obviously based only on the fact that both the realistic novel and the courtly romance are designated, in most European languages, by the same word.[6]

If the family sagas could be considered neither fiction nor historical truth – such concepts did not exist, there were only the concepts of "truth" and "falsehood" – then it must be assumed that they were considered either simply "falsehood" or simply "truth", truth including what we think of as fiction. The first possibility is improbable. In the famous description of the feast at Reykjahólar, "lying sagas" (and this is the only place in Old Icelandic literature where "lying sagas" are mentioned) is the term applied to typical "sagas of olden times" (*fornaldarsögur*) – works abounding in stereotyped fantastic adventures, obviously with no pretensions to truth. It was certainly not applied to the family sagas, works which basically have the appearance of truth, even from our modern point of view. Considering the beliefs and superstitions of the people of the thirteenth century, the family sagas were, of course, absolutely plausible. As is well known, the family sagas were used as reliable sources by those who, as they themselves declared, wanted to be "truthful", and whom modern investigators trust as "historians". This applies first and foremost to Sturla Þórðarson, who wrote such universally recognized "historical" works as *Íslendinga saga* in *Sturlunga saga, Hákonar saga Hákonarsonar,* and *Landnámabók.*[7]

The people of the thirteenth century could not distinguish historical truth from fiction in the family sagas not only because these concepts were unknown to them, but also because they did not, of course, possess the techniques of modern research. These techniques permit modern scholars to distinguish history from fiction, but at the same time apparently lead them to forget that the Icelanders of the thirteenth century did not read family sagas in special reading rooms where modern scholarly literature and all the editions of the Old Icelandic texts were at hand.

Must one not assume, however, that although the audience or readers of the family sagas accepted them simply as truth – as did everyone in Iceland right down to the most recent times – those who wrote these sagas knew that they were not true and consciously tried to deceive their readers by giving to the fiction as much appearance of truth as possible? Such an assumption is refuted, however, by the fact that it was particularly the saga writers – and most especially Sturla Þórðarson – who obviously accepted the family sagas as truth; they cited these sagas as reliable sources, and they must have known what the authors considered their own works to be.

A literary work is not something in and by itself, but something in which a certain interpretation is implicit. A work of conscious artistic invention is as a rule intended to be understood as artistic invention. But the family sagas obviously do not belong among such works. If such a work is accepted as truth in the proper sense of the word, as sometimes happens with people who are inexperienced in literature, then it has not fulfilled its proper function and has not been comprehended. If a literary work of conscious fiction is intended to be taken as actual truth, then it is a hoax, a relatively rare form of artistic invention. The family sagas obviously do not belong to this type of work either. Fiction in the sagas is, so to speak, "latent" fiction, fiction which the saga creators regarded as permissible, remaining within the limits of truth. Syncretic truth, since it was the only possible form of truth, had to be considerably broader than either of the truths of modern man. It did, after all, include things which, from the modern point of view, are only plausible, artistic truth and not real truth.

For the modern man everything told of the past is of necessity either historical truth or artistic truth. It is therefore very difficult for him to imagine truth which is neither the one nor the other, nor anything in between. But an idea of the attitude of saga writers to their narrative material, and an idea of the degree of their freedom with what seemed to them to be truth, may be given by accounts of the same event presented in two different sagas, prose paraphrases of verses cited in a saga, and different versions of the same saga. Still more significant are parallel sagas about the same Norwegian king – different versions of what was regarded as "the same saga", for example the various sagas of Saint Olaf, including Snorri Sturluson's saga in *Heimskringla*. It is obvious that Snorri considered his account to be truth rather than free invention, in spite of the fact that he, as has been established, invented dialogue, speeches, details of everyday life, the background of events, and psychological motivation, and introduced characters or literary motifs which seemed plausible to him and were consequently permissible within the bounds of truth. Clearly, the same kind of latent fiction was already present in his sources, written or oral. It is also clear that, although successive retellings of the same material were preserved only in the kings' sagas, owing to their special significance, the family sagas must contain similar latent fiction in so far as they are also syncretic truth.[8]

An idea of what constitutes syncretic truth may be given also by vestiges of this truth, widespread even in modern life, for example in the transmission of an everyday conversation, or in an everyday account by an eyewitness –

accounts laying claim to truth but of course always containing a certain amount of invention (admittedly not necessarily artistic invention). Indeed, no conversation can be reproduced exactly, as real truth, unless it has been tape-recorded. No eyewitness can mentally record all the details of an event, and people often see or hear what they want to see or hear, rather than what actually took place. An especially large amount of fiction is contained in everyday accounts of dreams. Dreams are usually so irrational and so poorly retained in the memory that it is impossible to recount their content with any degree of truthfulness. Moreover, any check is impossible. It is therefore not surprising that in literature, too, dreams as a rule are very conventionalized and not at all like dreams people actually have. In the family sagas, for instance, dreams are perhaps the most conventionalized element of all. They are always prophetic, are always accompanied by the same external manifestations (such as "he tossed in his sleep"), and contain traditional symbols which vary little from dream to dream and from saga to saga. Nevertheless, dreams in the sagas were undoubtedly accepted as truth. To the modern man they seem obvious literary invention, but this is only because in our time other conventions prevail in accounts of dreams, and the norms of what is permissible within the bounds of truth are not the same as those in early Icelandic society.[9]

Ascribing our modern ideas of literature and literary genres to people in ancient Iceland, modern scholars usually consider the family sagas somehow just as distinctly delimited as the literary genres of our time, and even frequently contrast these sagas regarded as "artistic literature" with certain other sagas regarded as "historical literature". Nothing like such a division existed, of course, in the mind of the medieval Icelander. Neither the family sagas nor other varieties of sagas – sagas of olden times, kings' sagas and bishops' sagas (all these designations originated only in modern times) – were regarded as separate literary genres. This is shown, for instance, by the fact that in the manuscripts they may be arranged indiscriminately, and also by the fact that the family sagas often contain passages which in no way differ from sagas of olden times or kings' sagas, while the kings' sagas contain passages which in no way differ from family sagas or sagas of olden times.[10]

All the Old Icelandic sagas are obviously connected by the fact that they are always narratives concerning the past – narratives regarded as truth, or at least with greater or less success passing for truth. The differences between the separate varieties of sagas arise only from the degrees of remoteness of this past and from the localizations of the actions narrated in them. The family sagas, i.e. sagas in which are recounted events of the first two centuries after the settlement of Iceland (tenth and eleventh centuries), differ from the sagas of olden times, i.e. sagas in which are recounted events preceding the settlement of Iceland, as well as from the sagas in which events of the twelfth and thirteenth centuries are narrated. But there is also a difference between the sagas in which events in Iceland are recounted (family sagas and some others) and the sagas in which events in other countries are told of (kings' sagas and sagas of olden times), and this second difference often overlaps the first. In other words, the sagas differ in that they tell of the remote, the less remote, and the recent past; and also in that they tell of events in Iceland, and of events outside Iceland. It is impossible to detect varieties of sagas that differ only in their treatment of the same content.

In place of the traditional division of the sagas, Sigurður Nordal, the head of the Icelandic school of philologists, has proposed dividing them according to the length of time between the events and their "recording". He puts them into three groups – "sagas about the remote past" (approximately until the year 850), "sagas about the past" (approximately 850–1100), and "sagas about contemporary time" (not earlier than approximately 1100). The family sagas would then form the second group, along with some of the kings' sagas. This division accurately reflects the fact that orientation in time is basic for differentiation among sagas. But the designation "sagas about contemporary time" is a misunderstanding, of course. It is not by any means the period contemporary to the writing that is described in these sagas, as is the case with the realistic novels of our time, but simply a more recent past than that described in the "sagas about the past". These sagas may also be the account of an eyewitness, but nevertheless they concern the past, not the present. Admittedly, the author of a realistic novel about the present may also write about what "happened in the recent past", but a novel is artistic truth, not syncretic truth. Therefore, when he writes "it happened in the past", the author of a novel does not mean that what is described *actually took place in the past,* but only that it *could take place in the present.* The sagas, on the other hand, are syncretic truth, and the writer of a saga about the recent past considered, of course, that the events he was describing actually took place in the past, and not merely that they could take place in his own time.

It is no mere chance that all sagas are narratives of the past. Narratives of the present in the sense described above could not yet exist, and this is one of the most outstanding differences between our modern ideas of literature and the old Icelandic ones. In narratives of the present, fiction is obvious, no matter how plausible it is. Therefore the fiction in narratives of the present cannot fail to be consciously realized, and a narrative of the present can be only artistic truth, not syncretic truth. This is why fiction – conscious invention intended to be recognized as such, though having the appearance of truth – came into literature together with narrative about the present. In thirteenth-century Iceland it was unknown. The process was completed in the realistic novel about contemporary time, i. e. not before the eighteenth century, and in Iceland not before the middle of the nineteenth century. Still later, conscious and deliberate fiction having the appearance of truth was put into narratives about the past; in other words, the historical novel appeared. The development of history as a scholarly discipline and of realistic novels of contemporary life made possible the rise of the historical novel. Thus essential antecedents for the historical novel were not only historical "non-novels" – scholarly investigations in the area of history – but also "non-historical" novels – realistic novels of contemporary life.

Most of the sagas about events of the recent past (twelfth and thirteenth centuries) in Iceland were collected in the compilation made about the end of the thirteenth century, known under the name *Sturlunga saga.*[11]

Sturlunga saga is distinguished from the family sagas by its greater attention to the compilation of facts – there are in it more than three thousand names alone, on nine hundred pages. For this reason it is usually considered "history", while family sagas are considered "literature". Drawing conclusions from this, some scholars even consider on the one hand that all dialogues in *Sturlunga saga* – and there are very many – are historical facts, apparently a tape-recording of conversations which actually took place; and on the other hand that characters in family sagas are artistic portrayals – in the guise of heroes of the tenth and eleventh centuries – of people who actually lived in the twelfth and thirteenth centuries, known to us from *Sturlunga saga*. They see the family sagas, that is, as *romans à clef*.[12]

In fact, however, the difference between *Sturlunga saga* and the family sagas has scarcely anything in common with the modern difference between history and belles-lettres. In our day, scholarly literature and belles-lettres differ from each other so much in treatment of material, in style and in vocabulary, that it is impossible not to distinguish one from the other – it is usually sufficient to read one line or simply to see the type of print, the format of the book, or the dust jacket. But for the Icelander of the thirteenth century both the sagas in *Sturlunga saga* and the family sagas were, of course, to an equal degree sagas and nothing else. The content of both is made up of feuds among Icelanders in the past. In both, battles and killings form dramatic peaks, which are preceded by prophetic dreams and the like. In both, strophes are cited, allegedly composed by saga-characters. Both contain references to oral tradition, such as "they tell", or "truthful people say". In both, genealogies and other detailed information are adduced, obviously fulfilling no artistic function. The same stereotyped expressions and conventional descriptions of woundings and killings are found in both. Finally, *Sturlunga saga* contains fiction of the same kind as the family sagas, i. e. latent fiction. All dialogues in *Sturlunga saga* are, of course, fiction, unless it is assumed that they are, by some miracle, a tape-recording. Especially obvious fiction is provided by dialogues in the heat of battle. The fact that some passages in *Sturlunga saga* were possibly written by an eyewitness does not, of course, exclude the possibility of fiction. Latent fiction is also comprised, of course, by all the omens, presentiments and prophetic dreams which precede dramatic events, as well as by the strophes uttered by characters from the other world who appear in dreams – and there are many such strophes in *Sturlunga saga.* In spite of the dryness and the compilation of facts, there are many deviations from factual truth in *Sturlunga saga*, and since in this work, as in the family sagas, feuds are depicted almost exclusively, while all the other sides of life are ignored, a rather one-sided picture of reality results.

From the point of view of modern scholarship, it is obvious that there is more epic stylization and dramatization of events in the family sagas than in *Sturlunga saga* – in other words, more fiction. But since this fiction in both the family sagas and *Sturlunga saga* was latent, the difference in its quantity could not be noticeable to the Icelander of the thirteenth century, unless in reading or listening to the saga he performed all the research work done by modern investigators – checking a chronology and so on against more reliable sources, and perhaps even undertaking excavations. But it would not be enough just to determine, as modern investigators do, whether these sagas represent belles-lettres or history – he would also have to be well-read in modern belles-lettres and scholarly literature.[13]

The difference in the quantity of fiction in family sagas (i. e. the sagas telling of the tenth and eleventh centuries) and in sagas telling of the more recent past is, of course, not at all due to the fact that the first are belles-lettres, while the second are history. Both are syncretic truth about the past. But it is obvious that the amount of fiction in the sagas is directly proportional to the interval between the events and the time of the writing of the sagas; and the reason for such a regularity of distribution of fiction in the sagas is also obvious – in oral tradition (and the presence of some oral tradition as the basis for the written sagas is undoubted) the amount of latent fiction increases as the events become further removed in time and less well known; in other words, as the possibility of accepting fiction as truth increases, or conversely, as the possibility of noticing fiction decreases.

The same regularity in the distribution of fiction is revealed if one compares family sagas with another large group of sagas – the sagas of olden times, narratives of events which as a rule belong to the age before the settlement of Iceland, or to the very remote past.[14]

The principal feature of typical sagas of olden times is the extensive use of folk-tale motifs and a folk-tale treatment of reality. In these sagas there are many giants and other supernatural creatures, tomb-dwellers protecting treasures, enchanted swords, various charmed objects, and so forth; and all the hero's wishes are always fulfilled: he always triumphs and achieves success, no matter the superiority of his enemies or their machinations; he always obtains a princess as a wife; and in general everything always ends happily for him.

It is beyond doubt, however, that the basis of this group of sagas is also syncretic truth. This is apparent first of all from the fact that the fairy-tale fantastic element, not connected with any definite age or country, by no means exhausts their content. Frequently there is reflected in them, although refracted through the prism of the magic tale, the Scandinavian reality of the age immediately preceding the settlement of Iceland – viking expeditions and the viking way of life, pagan beliefs, and clan and tribal feuds. The action in these sagas is frequently localized in the real world – in Norway, Sweden, Denmark, or England. Usually, considerably more names are mentioned in them than are necessary in a folk tale, and many of the people mentioned in these sagas are real historical personages. In general these sagas have something in common with family sagas – there are many genealogies in them, admittedly often fantastic ones, and feuds play a large part in them. As a rule these sagas in their looseness of composition are closer to family sagas than to folk tales with their compositional compactness. Frequently these sagas consist wholly of stereotyped motifs strung together. It is also characteristic that when the action in a family saga takes place in the age preceding the settlement of Iceland, the family saga is, as it were, transformed into a saga of olden times – fairy-tale motifs appear, verisimilitude disappears, scales of measurement become fantastic, and even the style changes, sentences become more rounded but have less content. Thus family sagas and sagas of olden times are, so to speak, the results of superimposing the same scale on two different realities – the past in Iceland, and the remote past outside Iceland.

All this applies to the typical sagas of olden times. But the best-known of these sagas, and apparently those reflecting the earliest stage of their development, are those based wholly or in part on heroic lays, preserved or hypothetical. It is beyond doubt that heroic lays constitute syncretic truth about events of the very remote past, which has been preserved in oral tradition. Such truth in poetic or prose form was probably also the prototype for sagas of olden times in general. But when events, narrated in oral tradition, recede into the very remote past, there is naturally more fiction in these narratives than when the narration concerns the more recent past; and therefore in these narratives a fairy-tale fantastic element very commonly finds a place. Thus the fairy-tale fantastic element is linked with what took place a very long time ago, and in any account of events of the very remote past it becomes an obligatory element. For this reason, evidently, a narrator could introduce fairy-tale motifs into a saga of events that took place before the settlement of Iceland and still count on the saga being believed. Admittedly, who-ever introduced these motifs into a saga was probably aware that he was inventing. It is characteristic that in precisely the sagas of olden times there appear extensive protestations that the account, in spite of the apparent lack of verisimilitude, is truthful, because people in remote times were stronger and larger, and life in general was subject to other laws.

In fact, in the sagas of olden times there is essentially no fantasy in the true sense of the word, no invention. The typical sagas of olden times break down entirely into absolutely stereotyped and mechanically strung together motifs. It is therefore not surprising that no form of author's self-consciousness ever shows itself in them. Nevertheless, no matter how stereotyped the fiction in them may be, in a certain sense it is closer to the fiction in modern novels than the fiction in family sagas is. This is because the lack of verisimilitude in the sagas of olden times probably made the fiction in them noticeable, i. e., it was no longer latent as in the family sagas, and consequently syncretic truth here gives way to an embryonic form of artistic truth. It was not without reason that King Sverrir called sagas of this kind "lying" and "most entertaining". Admittedly, the "lying" quality of these sagas was hardly obvious to everybody – belief in the supernatural was general, and trust in the written word was very great.

Actually, the magical fairy tale represents dissolution of syncretic truth and an incipient form of artistic truth. Indeed, the magical tale as a rule lays no claim to truthfulness, and consequently the fiction in it is consciously realized as such. Naturally, such an incipient form of artistic truth cannot fail to be obvious fiction, that is, fairy-tale fantasy, since otherwise it would be indistinguishable from syncretic truth. It is also natural that the incipient artistic truth arises as a sort of negative quantity. It is considered frivolous invention, absurd fable, something not deserving serious attention. Hence the disdain for the fairy tale, characteristic of ages when syncretic truth predominates, and expressed in the famous words of *Óláfs saga Tryggvasonar* by the monk Oddr: "It is better to listen to this [the history of a Norwegian king] for one's amusement than to tales about a stepmother [fairy tales in which a wicked stepmother figures], which are told by shepherds, and about which it is not known whether they are true."

The writing of sagas of olden times was begun, as is well known, later than that of all the other sagas – not before the middle of the thirteenth century and, for the most part, considerably later. For this reason it might be and has been assumed that this variety of sagas represents a later stage of development as compared with family sagas and others. The appearance of sagas of olden times has been looked upon as the result of a loss of a sense of reality or feeling for history, as a kind of decline and degeneration. Thanks, however, to one bit of evidence, preserved by chance and still not refuted, the existence of this variety of sagas in oral tradition as early as the beginning of the twelfth century is beyond doubt – according to *Þorgils saga ok Hafliða* in *Sturlunga saga,* a typical saga of olden times was narrated at a feast at Reykjahólar in 1119. Somewhat later, Saxo Grammaticus heard such sagas from a certain Icelander and he seems to have regarded them as true, inasmuch as he used them in his *Gesta Danorum.* Thus the later appearance of these sagas in written form does not show they were a later stage of development in comparison with other saga types, but rather it attests only to their lesser importance in the eyes of the people of the time, owing to their abundance of fairy-tale fantasy – disdain of this fantasy was, as has been stated, characteristic of the age. On the other hand, this does not of course exclude the fact that the popularity of the fairy-tale sagas in the post-classical period in Iceland – paralleling the spread of the courtly romance in other European countries – in fact marked the process of dissolution of the single – i. e. syncretic – truth, and the development of incipient artistic truth in the form of fairy-tale fantasy.

A large group of sagas – the kings' sagas – is also distinguished from family sagas, not by a different treatment of the same material, but by the material itself. But here the same scale is superimposed upon a reality differently situated not in time, but in space. Kings' sagas tell of events which took place in countries with kings, countries outside Iceland, chiefly Norway. The placing of these events in time is most frequently the same as in the family sagas, and the kings' sagas are closest to the family sagas both in the character of the truth presented in them and in their style. And in those parts of kings' sagas telling of Icelanders – the so-called *Íslendinga þættir* – they are in no way different from family sagas. For this reason, the *Íslendinga þættir* are usually included in editions of the family sagas. It is natural also that when kings' sagas tell of events preceding the settlement of Iceland and of legendary or mythical times, they are closest to sagas of olden times, while sagas telling of thirteenth-century kings are closest to *Sturlunga saga* and similar sagas.[15]

In one way, however, the kings' sagas differ essentially from sagas telling of events within Iceland – the kings' sagas tell of events in a country where, in contrast to Iceland, there was a state in the true sense of the word, state power concentrated in the hands of one man. The narrative material in these sagas is knit together by the fact that it concerns a state or its head, the king, and his rule. In family sagas the subject described – a feud between members of Icelandic society – is fully encompassed, all participants in the feud are mentioned and all events connected with it. But in kings' sagas the description is much less complete – naturally not everything connected with the reign of a given king, nor everything that takes place in his kingdom during his reign, can be encompassed, and therefore a selection of facts is inevitable. Thus, there is in the kings' sagas the embryo, so to speak, of historical truth; these sagas are closer to the historical truth of our time, and to history as a scholarly discipline, than the family sagas are – indeed, history also implies a selective description of the reality of the past, because of the impossibility of encompassing it in all its living fullness.

Admittedly, historians of Old Icelandic literature, regarding the contrast between history and literature as ages old, frequently refer some of the kings' sagas to "history" while denying this honor to others on the grounds that they contain more fiction. But in reality a greater or lesser degree of fiction (from the modern viewpoint) is, of course, by no means evidence that these sagas belong to two different genres. It is rather the result of natural fluctuations within the limits of syncretic truth, conditioned by the individual inclinations of the saga-writers. What seems to be the scholarly quality of a given saga is the manifestation of the personal inclinations of the saga-writer – his distrustfulness, his caution, and so on – and is by no means a characteristic of the genre. It is a completely different matter in our time, when a scholarly quality, or rather a pseudo-scholarly quality, may be simply the result of following a certain model, and not at all a manifestation of the personal inclinations of the author. In our day, in order to write a scholarly work, it is by no means necessary to possess the talents of a scholar. On the contrary, the fewer original thoughts, the easier, usually, to write a scholarly work: all one has to do is to follow a certain form – cite other authors a bit more, make use of special terms a bit more, and express oneself in as complex a manner as possible.

Kings' sagas also differ from family sagas and sagas of olden times in that the authors are in many cases known. For example, it is known that a certain Eiríkr Oddsson wrote a lost saga about Norwegian kings under the title of *Hryggjarstykki*, the abbot Karl Jónsson wrote *Sverris saga*, the monks Oddr Snorrason and Gunnlaugr Leifsson wrote sagas about King Óláfr Tryggvason, the priest Styrmir Kárason wrote *Óláfs saga helga,* Snorri Sturluson wrote *Heimskringla,* and his nephew Sturla Þórðarson wrote *Hákonar saga Hákonarsonar.* This naming is apparently due, on the one hand, to the fact that conscious authorship appeared first of all in the sagas representing incipient historical truth. But it is also probably due, on the other hand, to the fact that, since the sagas concerned kings – and in the case of the two Olafs, also propagators of Christianity – they were written in the interests of the monarchy and church, and upon the writers fell a reflection from the aureole which surrounded monarchy and church in the eyes of the people of the time. Indeed, in the family sagas also, and especially in *Laxdœla saga,* common means of exalting a hero are to provide eulogies uttered by a Norwegian king about him.

In conclusion, a word about truth in the bishops' sagas. These sagas tell of the Icelandic church in the person of its head, the bishop. But the church was Iceland's closest analogue to an organized state. Therefore, as in the king's sagas, the scope is smaller and more selective. Moreover, since these sagas tell of the recent past (the first bishop of Iceland was consecrated in 1056), these sagas are drier and contain more compilation of fact than the family sagas.[16]

But the special characteristic of bishops sagas is the tendency to publish as the truth whatever in the church's interest was to be considered the truth. In *Guðmundar saga Arasonar* there is the following naively revealing reasoning behind this new form of truth: "Everybody knows that everything good said about God and His saints is the truth; that is why it is good to believe the good, and bad to believe the bad, even if the latter is true, and worst of all to believe what is badly lied". In other words, truth was what was advantageous for the church. This new truth also crops up here and there in kings' sagas. For example, in Styrmir's *Óláfs saga helga* there is a statement to the effect that even the untrustworthy should be considered as the truth if it promoted Olaf's glorification. But the most obvious manifestation of this new form of truth is found in the so-called miracles (Icelandic *jarteikn,* literally "sign", "token"). These are most abundantly represented in the bishops' sagas. Accounts of the fulfilment of the wishes of anyone who appealed to a saint for help – a gravely ill person recovered, emitting a wonderful aroma; a blind person regained his sight; a deaf man began to hear; the weather improved; a cow calved ahead of time; a starving man succeeded in catching many fish; a lost object was found – passed for truth because, of course, to believe in them seemed something good, and not to believe in them seemed something bad. Good seemed to be whatever was in the best interests of the church, and bad – whatever ran counter to its interests. In other words, the purpose of these accounts was the glorification of the church in the person of its saint. The spread of this new form of truth – "ecclesiastical truth", as it were, or, since in Iceland the church was the state in embryo, "state truth" – is the basic contribution of Christianity in the area of conceptions of truth. This new truth subsequently bursts into luxuriant bloom everywhere, growing with the advancing strength of the church and the state. In comparison with the syncretic truth of the sagas, this new truth – which was actually not so much truth as falsification of truth – was a great regression (unless, of course, one considers the perfection of methods of falsification of truth also a kind of progress).

Thus from the point of view of the history of conceptions of truth, the kings' sagas and the bishops' sagas represent a later stage of development than the family sagas. It is also beyond question that both kings' sagas and bishops' sagas, to a considerably greater degree than family sagas, show the influence of medieval European literature, works of historiography, ecclesiastical biographies, and lives of saints. In spite of this, the opinion has in recent times prevailed among scholars that family sagas originated under the influence of kings' sagas. The principal argument in support of this opinion is that the oldest preserved kings' sagas were written before the oldest of the preserved family sagas – the former in the seventies and eighties of the twelfth century, and the latter probably not before the beginning of the thirteenth century. It is quite possible that the writing of kings' sagas was begun earlier than that of family sagas – after all, the aureole surrounding the Norwegian kings in the eyes of the Icelanders made them seem more important. It is also true that oral family sagas could not be preserved verbatim in written form – they could not be recorded as oral tradition can be recorded in our day. But it does not by any means follow that oral family sagas did not exist, or that the written family sagas could be created except on the basis of oral sagas. The principal content of the family sagas is feuds among Icelanders in the tenth and eleventh centuries. How could information concerning such feuds be preserved from the tenth and eleventh centuries? In oral biographical dictionaries or some other kind of oral reference books? Apparently something of the sort is tacitly assumed by those who doubt the existence of oral family sagas and speak vaguely of "oral tradition" in which this information might have been preserved. It is perfectly obvious that in oral tradition information concerning feuds among the Icelanders in the tenth and eleventh centuries (the oldest written family sagas apparently belong to the beginning of the thirteenth century) could be preserved only in the form of sagas, i. e. in narratives representing syncretic truth which, while containing more or less latent fiction, were nevertheless accepted as real truth. In such a case, the specific characteristic of the written family sagas is that they represent syncretic truth as much as their oral prototypes did.

Where are the limits of the human personality?

> What's Montague? It is nor hand, nor foot,
> Nor arm, nor face, nor any other part
> Belonging to a man.
>
> *Shakespeare*

The peculiar character of the limits set to human personality within the Icelandic society described in the family sagas is manifested most distinctly in the identification of oneself with one's kinsmen. This follows from the duty of avenging them: from the unconquerable, elemental power with which this duty imposed itself on the individual, overcoming in him all egoistic feelings, including the fear of death. This duty formed the basic motive power in any feud, and feuds constitute the principal matter in the family sagas. But the spiritual world of the people among whom these sagas arose is shown not only – and not so much – in *what* is told in them. Family sagas tell of the comparatively remote past – about what was already perhaps anachronistic – and it is not known just what in them is historical truth and what is fiction. But any family saga accurately reflects the spiritual world of the people it originated among in *how* it tells about this past.

Modern investigators of family sagas as a rule make the tacit assumption that each of them had exactly the same kind of author as literary productions of our day. Just as an author of today writes a novel, so the "author" of a saga wrote his work. He was, in the full meaning of the word, its creator; he distinguished it from his sources; he expressed in it his feelings and views; and he demonstrated his art in it and naturally understood that he was an "author". This seems the assumption made by modern investigators. Such an assumption is absolutely necessary, of course, for anyone seeking to discover when and how a saga writer created a given family saga – what his sources were, who he was, what constitutes his art – in other words, for anyone investigating it in the way these sagas have usually been investigated in recent times. The search for an author of a saga becomes especially easy if it is assumed that he constantly gave indications about himself as the author to a future scholar, by alluding to events from his own life, to his surroundings, or to others of his works; or by consistently using the same words and expressions. If one comes to believe in the wonder-working nature of counting such words and expressions, the search for authors of family sagas becomes simple and entertaining, like a child's game. On the other hand, if one does not accept this assumption, all investigations of family sagas from the point of view of when and how they were created by their supposed authors, what the sources of these sagas were, who their authors were, and so on – in other words, the greater part of all modern research into these sagas – become completely senseless. It is therefore understandable why this assumption is always made by modern investigators, in spite of the fact that it flagrantly contradicts everything that is known about authorship relative to the family sagas, and indeed relative to Old Icelandic sagas in general, and contradicts what investigations based on this assumption inevitably disclose.[17]

The question of *what* the family sagas were thought to be is the reverse side of the question of *who* the saga writers thought themselves to be. If the person who writes considers what is written to be his own invention, by the same token he considers himself the author of what is written. But if he thinks he is simply transmitting the truth, how can he regard himself as its author? Syncretic truth is what is thought of as simply truth, something given, not created. Thus syncretic truth, or the lack of distinction between historical and artistic truth, inevitably implies the absence of the consciousness of authorship. And the lack of consciousness of authorship is the lack of consciousness of the limits of the human personality.

The lack of conscious authorship relative to the Icelandic sagas is made most evident by linguistic data. In Old Icelandic there were no words to express the concepts "author" or "authorship", and consequently these concepts did not exist for people in old Icelandic society. The Icelandic word *höfundur* ("author") appeared only in the eighteenth century. Such words as "writer", "novelist", or "historian" – words in which authorship is understood – are abundantly represented in all modern European languages, but were totally lacking in Old Icelandic. There were only such words as *ritari* (from *rita,* "to write") meaning "scribe"; *sagnamaðr* (from *saga* and *maðr*, "man") and *sagnameistari* (*meistari,* "master"), both meaning "he who knows sagas", "a good saga-teller"; *fræðimaðr* (from *fræði,* "knowledge", "wisdom") meaning "he who knows things", "a wise man".[18]

It was also in reality impossible to express descriptively the concept "author" as "one who has composed, written", and suchlike. In Old Icelandic there was no word with the meaning "to compose" in a literary sense. The Icelandic word *semja,* "to compose", acquired this meaning only in modern times, and the word *dikta,* "to compose", was used only of works in Latin. As for the Old Icelandic verbs *rita* (or *ríta*) and *skrifa,* both meaning "to write", their meaning differed drastically from the meanings of corresponding verbs in modern European languages. The fact is that these Old Icelandic verbs never implied the activity of an author as something distinguished from writing down, copying, or rewriting. In other words, the meaning "to compose", "to be the author", was not developed in them. If, as is clear from the context, they do refer to a man who is supposed to have actually been the author, it is only an isolated instance of their use in a meaning that in itself does not imply the activity of an author, whereas in the English verb "to write", for example, the meaning "to compose (in a literary sense)" is distinctly set apart from its other meanings. This is apparent from the fact that this meaning can be expressed by other words, such as "to compose" or "to be the author", and by the fact that this verb is also found in contexts where only the activity of an author can be understood, not writing in the original meaning of the word, as in sentences like "Who wrote this novel?" or "This author has not written anything for a long time". Naturally, the meanings "to compose" or "to be the author" could develop in the Old Icelandic verb with the basic meaning of "to write" only if its direct object could be the designation of a literary work, implying conscious authorship – words with such meanings as "novel", "novella", "article", or "investigation" – or if its subject could be a word with the meaning "author": in other words, if in Old Icelandic one could say such things as "He wrote a novel", or "The author is writing". But, as has already been said, such words did not exist in Old Icelandic. What has been said about the Old Icelandic verbs meaning "to write" also holds true for the Old Icelandic verbs *segja fyrir* or *sitja yfir,* "to dictate", and *setja saman,* "to compile". In a number of instances they refer to people who, it is supposed, were "authors". But the meaning "to be the author" was obviously not distinguished in these verbs from the meanings "to dictate" and "to compile" respectively.

The lack of consciousness of authorship in relation to the family sagas also follows from their consistent anonymity – the writers never named themselves, and nobody else named them. The consistent anonymity of the family sagas has been variously explained by the "modesty" of their authors, the "absence in them of any urge toward originality", the "indifference to the rights of an author", "Christian humility", or simply "tradition". But the question arises how is one to explain the "modesty" of the authors of the family sagas, their "indifference to the rights of authorship", and the rest. Obviously, by a special attitude toward authorship, unlike ours, and by undeveloped conceptions of authorship – in other words, by its unconscious nature.

Admittedly it might also be assumed that the consistent anonymity of the family sagas is due to chance. After all, the authors of certain other sagas – chiefly some of the kings' sagas – are known. But this is just the point – precisely in those instances where the saga author is supposedly known, the lack of conscious authorship is most evident. As a rule, a saga writer is supposedly known because in some Old Icelandic literary monument it is written that the saga was "written", "dictated", or "compiled" by so-and-so. But, as has already been pointed out, the meaning of these words is not at all identical with that of such modern expressions as "to compose" or "to be the author". Moreover, the very bit of information that so-and-so "wrote" or "compiled" a certain work is given, not at all with the purpose of attributing it to a definite author but from completely different motives – for example in order to explain something written by someone else, thereby giving his name. Finally, all the Old Icelandic works whose authors are supposedly known – such as Abbot Karl Jónsson's *Sverris saga*, Snorri Sturluson's *Heimskringla,* and Sturla Þórðarson's *Hákonar saga Hákonarsonar* and *Íslendinga saga* – obviously lay claim to being truth rather than their authors' invention, i. e., they are syncretic truth, or truth in which lack of conscious authorship is implicit.

All the Old Icelandic words which might still be suspected, in certain cases, of implying authorship, such as *rita* or *skrifa* ("to write") and *setja saman* ("to compile"), are obviously no older than the art of writing. It presumably follows that, before the beginnings of writing, there was no possibility at all of expressing the attribution of a work to a definite author. It is curious, however, that this is true only in relation to prose works. The words *skáld* ("author of verse") and *yrkja* ("to be the author of verses") undoubtedly existed long before the introduction of writing. Thus for a long time the words meaning "author of verses" and "to be the author of verse" existed, while there were no words that meant just "author" and "to be the author". This obviously means that authorship became conscious in poetry much earlier than in prose. On the other hand, it is beyond doubt that syncretic truth predominated also in skaldic poetry, and this to an even greater degree than in the sagas. The skalds obviously considered that they were transmitting simply the truth and not their invention in their verses, particularly the eulogistic lays. This is apparent, for example, in Snorri Sturluson's famous words: "We recognize as truth everything that is said in these verses concerning forays or battles of kings, since although the skalds customarily praise most that ruler before whom they stand, not one skald would dare attribute to him that which is a lie and an invention, as would be known to all who heard it, including the ruler himself."

Thus it turns out that syncretic truth also prevailed in works which were obviously the product of conscious authorship – in the poetry of the skalds – and this apparently contradicts the thesis that syncretic truth implies lack of conscious authorship. But if the character of authorship in skaldic poetry is examined, the predominance of syncretic truth in it proves on the contrary to be one of the most important pieces of evidence in favor of the thesis set out above. The extreme formalism, characteristic of skaldic poetry, is undoubtedly an indication that creativity in this poetry could be directed only toward form, but not toward content. The content in skaldic poetry, being syncretic truth, could not be the product of conscious authorship. The skald obviously regarded himself as the author only of the form, not of the content. Thus authorship in skaldic poetry was not conscious authorship in the modern sense.

The absence of conscious authorship, of course, does not imply the absence of authorship, or of creativity in general. But it undoubtedly implies a special kind of creativity. Authorship in relation to works embodying syncretic truth had to be something completely different from authorship in the modern sense. Therefore, if the word "author" is used in relation to the family sagas, it ought perhaps to be placed in quotation marks. Authorship was manifested in the family sagas primarily in latent fiction, or fiction which the saga "authors" permitted themselves while remaining within the limits of what was thought to be truth. Therefore it was not conscious invention or conscious creativity. Latent fiction was, of course, artistic creativity, but since it was not consciously such, it was not given the significance which the modern man ascribes to it. Therefore, the saga writer, as well as the saga narrator, did not necessarily strive to introduce latent fiction into the saga – to be its "author". In this way, the creativity of the saga writer or narrator could be considerably less than an author's creativity in the modern sense. It could even approach zero, in which case the saga writer was simply a more or less accurate recorder if he had an oral source, or copyist if his source was written.

In our day, the boundaries between transcription, copying, editing, compiling, and composing are as a rule quite distinct. The absence of conscious authorship implies a less distinct realization of the bounds of the human personality. If the writer was not conscious of his function as an author, he naturally could not separate it from what we call recording, copying, compiling, editing, reworking, and the like. Consequently, such words as "recorder", "copyist", "compiler", and "editor" ought also to be used in quotation marks when applied to the family sagas, since their meanings in this case would differ from those now usual. It is evident, from a comparison of various copies or versions of the same family saga, that the "recorder" or "copyist" could also perform the function of an editor or an author – change the style, make abridgements or additions, and introduce latent fiction, in the shape of fictitious dialogues for example. But on the other hand, in a number of instances it is evident that the so-called "author" simply copied. Thus authorship in the family sagas is something extremely indefinite. Admittedly, the existence of a clear-cut boundary between "author" and "copyist", usually assumed by modern investigators, is allegedly proved by the fact that the most popular sagas, especially *Njáls saga,* have been preserved in numerous manuscripts which are very similar to one another – supposedly copies of one "author's original". But another explanation is also possible: in the case of a popular text the copying could be accompanied by minimal creativity. The existence of an "author's original" in the modern sense – and this expression has no sense other than the modern one – is still less probable in relation to the other family sagas.

In the introductions to the separate volumes of the best modern edition of the family sagas (*Íslenzk fornrit*), introductions which are usually complete investigations, the authors always proceed on the assumption that each saga had an author in the modern sense, and try to determine his sources. But it is always apparent from the facts given that these "sources" were by no means sources in the modern sense. Inasmuch as the content of the saga was syncretic truth, the saga would appear to be identical with the sources, even if it were expanded with latent fiction. Moreover, the dependence of the "author" on his sources proves in a number of instances to be much greater than would have been the case had he been an author in the modern sense – quite often apparently, he simply copies from his source, without realizing the distinction between authorship and copying or recording. The "author" then proves rather to be anyone who has introduced some sort of creative contribution into the source, or into the source of the source, and so on, oral source included. It is evident that, although the intensity of creativity could be different with different people or even with the same person, the general character of this creativity, i. e. its unconscious nature and so forth, was the same in oral tradition. Of course, the introduction of the art of writing ultimately brought about a certain change in conceptions of truth, the role of the personality, and so on. But these conceptions are deeply rooted in the human psyche, and any change in them could only be very gradual. And in the Icelandic society of the period when the sagas were being written, these conceptions were undoubtedly much closer to those which had predominated before the introduction of writing than they were to modern ones.

Study of modern folklore shows that an author's activity always has a place in oral tradition, even in the fairy tale – the most traditional and stereotyped folklore genre – but the intensity of this activity varies, and may be negligible. The creativity of the author must also have had a place throughout the time when what were to be sources of family sagas were only oral. Perhaps it was then in general more intensive than after the introduction of writing, since the impossibility of fixing a tale in writing made for greater freedom in creativity. In any event, it is impossible to establish the extent of the author's contribution, not only in the case of lost oral sagas, but also in the case of preserved written sagas – indeed, their sources cannot in a single instance be fully known.

The problem of the origin of the family sagas, which has long agitated the scholarly world, is essentially also the problem of the limits of authorship. It is curious that in the last century and a half, scholarly opinion concerning the origin of the family sagas has oscillated like a pendulum from one extreme to the other, and there are signs that the pendulum is continuing to swing. In the first half of the last century the opinion established itself that the family sagas were the written record of oral tradition. But in the second half of the century, the theory (later called the "book-prose theory") gained ground that formless oral traditions were collected in the thirteenth century by "wise men" and given the form of the saga. Thus, according to this theory, the family sagas were written works created by their authors. At the beginning of our century, to replace the "book-prose theory" came the theory (called the "free-prose theory") that not only the content but also the form of the family sagas took shape before they were written down, and thus these sagas, with certain reservations with regard to the longest and most complex in composition, were the recording of oral tradition, possibly even verbatim in a number of instances. From the 1930s there was a return to the theory which maintains that the family sagas were not the writing down of oral tradition but written works created by their authors, and this theory soon gained ascendancy. Attempts have, however, been made, and especially recently, to find some intermediate solutions. But upon close examination, it always turns out that whoever advances a supposedly intermediate solution actually adheres to one of the two extremes – sometimes one, sometimes the other, sometimes simply eclectically combining them.[19]

The weak side of the "free-prose theory" is that it assumes on the one hand the existence of "recorders" like modern recorders of folklore, and on the other hand, in regard to oral sagas, "authors" like modern authors. But the "book-prose theory" ignores to a much greater degree the character of authorship in the family sagas. It assumes that we know what cannot be exactly known – the extent of an author's contribution to a saga – and assumes that we do not know what is perfectly well known – the form of "oral tradition which served as the source for the written saga" (as the partisans of the "book-prose theory" bashfully call the oral saga). It is obvious that this oral tradition, being syncretic truth, could not help being a narrative with a greater or smaller admixture of latent fiction – in other words, a saga. We must investigate only what is known and ignore what is unknown, say the partisans of the "book-prose theory", and thereby in fact propose to ignore the origin of written sagas in general. They devote special attention to the dating of the separate sagas, i. e. to differences which are very petty in comparison to the differences between the conceptions of a thirteenth-century Icelander and those of a modern man. This last difference they do not notice at all, for the reason that it is all too obvious.

Nevertheless, in dating the separate sagas, modern investigators have not succeeded in attaining convincing results. The fact is that the criteria used in dating family sagas – such as borrowings from other written sagas, mention of persons or events more recent than the time of the narrative in the saga, other reflections of the time of the writing in the saga, and greater or lesser "maturity" of style – are based on the false assumption that the saga authors were, so to speak, authors of the same kind as modern professional writers. And borrowings from other written sagas (the most popular criterion for dating sagas) assume, moreover, that the saga author was not only a professional writer, but also a professional literary critic, attentively following all new works in the field of his specialization and reading them immediately upon their appearance. The methods of modern investigators of the family sagas are essentially based on a vicious circle – acknowledgment of the family sagas as works written by authors similar to modern professional writers assumes an evaluation of these sagas in accordance with modern criteria, but such an evaluation in turn assumes the acknowledgment of them as works written by authors similar to modern professional writers.[20]

The equating of the author of a family saga with a modern author is often based on the assumption that this saga bears an "individual stamp". Generally speaking, there are immeasurably more features of language, style and manner common to *all* the family sagas than there are features which might be taken to give an individual stamp to any single saga. But even if it is possible to detect in a saga something like an individual stamp, it is impossible – considering the character of authorship in the sagas, its lack of distinction from retelling, copying, and the like – to establish to what degree this stamp is really that of an "author".

It is asserted that the tastes, interests, or views of the authors show in individual sagas – in *Laxdœla saga* interest in finery and any sort of magnificence, in *Njáls saga* interest in legal formulas and belief in fate, in *Eyrbyggja saga* interest in pagan customs and sorcery and apparitions. But features characteristic of individual works are also possible, of course, in the most traditional folklore – there, too, individual works may well bear the traces of the tastes or sympathies of the narrators. Similar features are also possible in a compilation held together by a common theme – in fact, the common theme itself implies certain interests or views. Obviously, however, features of this kind do not form an author's personality – as it were the aggregate of psychological characteristics which consistently show through the whole work – or the author's point of view, i.e. a point of view which consistently runs through the whole work, organizing it into a unified whole and determining in particular the temporal perspective. Such an author's point of view cannot be detected even in the Old Icelandic works whose authors are apparently known to us, such as *Heimskringla* or the *Younger Edda,* unless, of course, one regards the absence of a consistent point of view as also a kind of consistent point of view. It is also characteristic that although *Heimskringla* and the *Younger Edda* are attributed to the same author – Snorri Sturluson – one can hardly detect any features common only to these two works. It would never have occurred to a single investigator to attribute these works to the same author, if there were not appropriate evidence of it (though in regard to *Heimskringla*, incidentally, this evidence has not been preserved).

Those who are regarded as the authors of Old Icelandic prose works never become, as authors, the objects of portrayal in Old Icelandic literature. Thus, although Snorri Sturluson is mentioned many times in *Íslendinga saga,* several times in *Hákonar saga Hákonarsonar,* and occasionally elsewhere, and a great deal is known about his participation in feuds, his property dealings, his trips to Norway, and the like, there is only one mention of his connection with the prose works of which he is considered the author. This is the very obscure reference in *Íslendinga saga*: "Sturla was then for long periods at Reykjaholt, and was very keen about getting books of sagas copied from the books that Snorri compiled." It is not known either what "books" are referred to, or what "compiled" means. Nonetheless, by comparing *Heimskringla* with its extant written sources, it is possible to establish some features of his authorship (although to what degree these features are characteristic of Snorri, and not generally of all those writing such works, is questionable). Thus, something is known of Snorri not only as a participant in feuds and so on, but also in part as an author of prose works. It is therefore understandable why the question whether Snorri also wrote *Egils saga* seems important and again and again attracts the attention of investigators. On the other hand, it is impossible to understand, even if one believes that the family sagas had the same kind of authors as modern novels have, what sense there is in trying to establish, at the cost of immense expenditure of effort and erudition – as has repeatedly been done recently – the name of a possible author of this or that saga, if nothing is known about the bearer of this name as an author.

The skalds are the only authors who are depicted in Old Icelandic literature as authors. This is of course due to the fact that the skalds were the only authors conscious of their authorship. But in the image presented in Old Icelandic literature the skalds are completely unlike poets in the modern sense. To be a skald did not mean possessing a certain turn of mind or spirit. To be a skald meant only having the ability to compose verses, being the master of verse form, i.e. possessing a characteristic which could be used to describe a person, just like such things as his height or the color of his hair. *Hallfreðar saga* gives a typical introductory description of a skald: "He was, from his youth, tall and strong, manly in appearance; he had somewhat slanting brows, a rather ugly nose, and dark hair which suited him. He was a good skald." And in *Gunnlaugs saga* there is the following introductory description of a skald: "He was tall, strong, and very handsome. He was a good skald." In such introductory descriptions it is said, as a rule, that so-and-so was "a good skald" or "a great skald" – i.e., he could compose good verses – but never simply that he was "a skald". Admittedly, the word "skald" (*skáld*) sometimes formed nicknames (Skáld-Hrafn, Skáld-Refr, Skáld-Þórir) but here too it designated a particular characteristic, similar to such traits as lameness or baldness, and not a special turn of mind. No matter whether the poetic composition was good or bad, or whether its author composed verses in general or only in the one single instance, its author could be called "skald". For this reason, in verse the word "skald" and its poetic equivalents were synonyms of the pronoun "I". The English word "poet" and its equivalents in modern European languages can refer to the author of prose, or even to a person who has never composed anything. It is possible, for example, to say, "He has the soul of a poet." In the same way, modern designations for poetry may apply to prose, and vice versa. For example, one may say, "In this novel there is much poetry," or "There is no poetry in this poem", or "This poem is simply prose." It was impossible to say anything of the kind in Old Icelandic. Under no circumstances could the word *skáld* refer to the author of prose or, in fact, to anyone who was not the author of verse. In the same way, the word "poetry" (*skáldskapr*) could apply only to verse. All this is a demonstration, on the one hand, of the fact that a sharply defined boundary lay between poetry and prose, between conscious and unconscious authorship; and on the other hand, of the fact that in poetry, authorship, as has already been stated, was conscious only in relation to form, not to content.

Those depicted in the sagas as the authors of verses, i.e. skalds, are revealed as individual personalities not through their poetic creativity or verses, but in exactly the same way as other persons mentioned in sagas. The direct descriptions of characters in sagas, like the introductory characterizations of the skalds given above, do not so much reveal the personality as attach to it, for life, a certain label. The qualities enumerated in these characterizations are generally rather standard. External qualities are, however, usually more individualized than internal ones, and at the same time external qualities correspond to some degree to internal ones. Thus, the word "tall" (*mikill*), which is encountered especially frequently, apparently implied also strength and courage. It is also characteristic that an important role is played by mention of the fact that a given man was liked or disliked – an evaluation of him which could not possibly be taken as the point of view of the author. Direct descriptions most frequently introduce a character; more seldom they are given in the middle of the account, at an especially important moment in the character's life; sometimes they are given at the end of a narrative about him. But direct descriptions are in general by no means obligatory in the sagas.[21]

A person is revealed in the family sagas not by direct characterization but through his relationships with other people. In fact, it is actually not individual persons who are depicted in the sagas, but certain kinds of relationships among people – breaking the peace, a feud and its causes, course and consequences. If there is no feud in any form, if there are no clashes, killings, battles or litigation, then there is no story in the saga. The internal world of the individual is never depicted for itself. The individual is never alone with himself; he never utters monologues, never analyzes his experiences, and never tells of them. He is revealed only in the way his relationships develop with other people in a feud. The circumstances of the feud are described in all their details; literally everything that people said is cited; everything having any connection with the feud is told. In this way, a mass of facts about the individual also comes out. At times everything said by him is reported in as much detail as if it were recorded on a tape-recorder, and the impression is created that it is the individual who is being depicted. But this is, of course, an illusion. In reality the abundance of facts reported in the family sagas concerning an individual participating in a feud is the result of the absence of interest in the individual personality for its own sake. The human personality was less distinct in people's minds.

Actually, interest in the individual first makes itself known in the bishops' sagas, and is manifested in immoderate and exaggerated eulogies of the moral perfections of the hero, the bishop. Thus the awakening of interest in individual personality led to a sharp decrease in the objectivity and truthfulness of its portrayal – when the individual became the object of portrayal, his moral evaluation appeared predominant in the foreground and obscured the objective facts.

The family sagas mention in all more than seven thousand persons; single sagas mention hundreds, long sagas many hundreds. In *Njáls saga* more than 700 persons are named. Some names are repeated many times in a single saga. In *Njáls saga,* for example, there are fifteen Þorkells, twelve Þórirs, seven Helgis, ten Grímrs, and fourteen Ketills. Often nothing is reported about the bearers of these names, other than their origins, nicknames, or homes. This abundance of names often causes difficulties for the modern reader, who is not accustomed to remembering names in such quantity. To a considerable degree, this abundance of names is due to the fact that the family sagas comprise syncretic truth, not artistic truth, and consequently these names are not an artistic device: they are not form, but content, as will be discussed in greater detail in the next chapter. The abundance of names in family sagas is also due to the inability to portray the human personality by itself, outside its relationships with other people, outside a feud, as was discussed above. But there is still another reason for the abundance of names in the family sagas – proper names were not then what they seem to us now.

For modern people, a personal name, even when it is at the same time a common noun (such as, for example, Faith or Hope), is a tag attached to its bearer, not internally connected with him and not forming an inseparable part of him. Even Shakespeare understood the nature of a man's name in precisely this way. "What's Montague?" says Juliet, "It is nor hand, nor foot, Nor arm, nor face, nor any other part Belonging to a man." Admittedly, the tendency to think of a name as motivated by the character or the external appearance of a person exists, even in our day. Some people think, for example, that a man is named John, Edward, or Thomas because it corresponds to his character, or vice versa, that a certain man should be named John because of his character or external appearance, although he is in fact named something else. Such notions vary from person to person, but may be constant for a given circle of people, and sometimes even for all the speakers of a given language. It is also known that in belles-lettres the characters' names are often felt to be motivated by their individual characteristics. A name can also in a certain sense create the character bearing it, as when an author has thought of the name of a literary character before he has thought out the character itself. All these, however, are only exceptional cases. In general, for the modern man proper names are tags devoid of any significance and serving only to distinguish their bearers. And this is especially obvious when nothing is known of the bearer of a given name. For a man nowadays such a name is an empty sound, ballast uselessly burdening memory. For this reason, people today are tired out by the enormous number of names which they find in the family sagas – after all, for the most part, little or nothing is known of their bearers.[22]

But for the man of the society in which the family sagas were created, names were apparently much less like tags that had no internal connection with their bearers. And this was not because the bearers of the names mentioned in the sagas were always familiar to the people, but because the connection of a name with its bearer was generally firmer and closer. In modern languages completely "disembodied" proper names are possible – names considered independently, whether or not they are attached to anything, listed in works on onomastics for example or in lists of recommended or usual personal names. In the society in which the family sagas originated all proper names were used only as "embodied", i.e., they were attached to definite objects. In any personal name some definite person was always implicit, even if nothing was known about this person except his most general characteristic – for example, the fact that he was an Icelander. Nonetheless, the name of this person had more content than the word "Icelander" did. The boundary between common and proper nouns was not fixed, and was completely different from that in modern languages. This is apparent, for example, from the very peculiar usage of certain proper nouns – about whose bearers nothing is known, other than their most general characteristic – as common nouns in skaldic poetry. Thus "fire of the Marne" (and nothing was known to the skalds about the Marne, except that it was a river somewhere) meant "fire of the river", i.e. "gold". This usage is not at all like the transformation of a proper into a common noun in modern European languages, where a proper noun designating a person possessing generally known characteristics easily serves to designate these characteristics, becoming, as it were, "disembodied" (thus the name Aristotle may acquire the meaning "a very intelligent man", for example). The "embodiment" of names was apparently much greater than in our day.

The most obvious manifestation of the greater "embodiment" of proper nouns is their role in the family sagas. Thousands of "embodied" proper nouns are given in these sagas – long genealogical series, long lists of names of concrete persons, hundreds of names of concrete places in Iceland. The genealogies are especially characteristic. To a modern man, unless he is a historian with very specialized interests, they seem simply ballast, a collection of empty sounds. But at one time they probably seemed to be the elements with maximum content in the sagas. It is also characteristic that if some person is mentioned in a family saga, his name is given without fail, no matter how episodic or insignificant a role he played. On the other hand, such expressions as "a certain man" are extremely rare in the family sagas. It is no less characteristic that the name of a person taking part in the action of a saga is, as a rule, introduced before, sometimes long before, it is told what comprises this person's participation in the saga action. The name was of itself so "embodied" that its mere mention meant the introduction of the person into the saga. The name was a part of the human personality – but this, of course, is not at all the same thing as became possible with the development of the state, when a title or rank at times becomes a part, even the major and basic part, of the human personality.

What is form and what is content?

> If I wanted to say briefly all that I intended to express by a novel, I would have to write the same novel as I wrote in the first place.
>
> *Lev Tolstoy*

In the family sagas a resemblance to modern realistic novels is often found, and it is customary to speak of their "realism", their "realistic quality", and so on. Thereby it is acknowledged that a miracle of literary history has occurred: in a period when the leading countries of medieval Europe were dominated by feudal and ecclesiastical ideology, dogmatism and scholasticism, and mannered and conventional literary genres, then at the northernmost edge of the inhabited world, on a remote island in the middle of the ocean, in a sparsely inhabited country where there was not one city, there suddenly began to appear literary works anticipating – by more than half a millennium! – the realistic literature of modern times, i. e. anticipating what was the result and crowning achievement of centuries of literary development. But is the "realism" in family sagas really the same thing as realism in modern literature? Of course not.

Realism in modern literature is artistic truth – in other words, verisimilar fiction, apprehended as art and not as truth in the proper sense of the word; while the family sagas constitute syncretic truth – fiction apprehended as truth in the proper sense of the word. Thus when one speaks of the "realism" of the sagas without stipulating that realism of a quite special kind is meant, one ascribes to these works something that was not in them and could not be in them. The realism of modern literature is to the realism of sagas as verisimilitude is to truth. Therefore, if the word "realism" is applied to sagas, it should be stipulated that it is, as it were, the "realism of truth" as distinguished from the "realism of verisimilitude" of modern times. When family sagas are taken to have the realism of verisimilitude, content is often being taken for form. The fact is that the very relationship of form and content in works representing syncretic truth does not correspond to modern conceptions in this area – what in the realism of verisimilitude is form may, in the realism of truth, be content, and vice versa.

The modern reader of the family sagas is most struck by the fact that they contain an enormous amount of various data – personal names, place names, and especially genealogies, which are obviously unnecessary for the development of the action or the description of the characters. What are these data – form or content? In works which are realistic in the modern sense of the word, the purpose of such data would be to impart verisimilitude to the narrative, making it similar to – but by no means identical with – a court record, a newspaper item, or other genres claiming to be truth in the proper sense of the word, rather than artistic truth. In other words, in the case of realism of verisimilitude such data would constitute an artistic device, an element of artistic form. An artistic device would then also be the author's admission that not all details are known to him, that this or that detail has slipped his mind, and the like. Such an admission would be an imitation of a conscientious transmission of truth. Those who take the family sagas for works which are realistic in the modern sense of the word – for fiction – must naturally also take all the data set forth in them as an artistic device. Authors who are most consistent in ignoring what constitutes truth in the sagas sometimes do just that. It is, however, characteristic that, although recently the family sagas have usually been interpreted as fiction, in current editions they are always annotated as if they were historical sources rather than artistic works – a chronological scale is set up, cross references are made, and information is given about persons and places mentioned in the saga. But it is absurd to annotate works of fiction in this way. How would it be if *Anna Karenina,* for example, were provided with such footnotes?

It is, of course, obvious that there are so-called "artistically dead elements", in the family sagas, i. e. data which not only fail to further the development of the action or the description of the characters, but also do not have the purpose of imparting verisimilitude to the saga. They are reported only because they were really regarded as truth and therefore entered the saga as an inseparable part of its content. In such a case, the information found in the sagas to the effect that this or that fact was unknown is not an artistic device, but simply conscientiousness in transmitting truth. When, in modern works on the family sagas, the content of a saga is set forth in the form of a synopsis, all the "artistically dead elements" are, of course, omitted and are consequently considered as something not entering into the content of the saga, i. e., they are considered elements of form. But to a man of the period in which the family sagas were created, it would probably have seemed that such a synopsis was simply absurd, and that it emasculated the saga and deprived it of content.

The style of the family sagas has been defined as "pure", "unconditional", or "absolute" prose. A primary characteristic of it is the absence of ornamentation or figures, even epithets, to say nothing of metaphors. Thus, minimal stylization is characteristic of the family sagas – minimal deviation from the manner in which language is used in living speech. In this prosaism there is undoubtedly a certain resemblance to the renunciation of rhetoric and figurativeness which, with the appearance of the realistic novels, became the characteristic feature of realistic literature in general. But this resemblance is purely external, of course. The prosaism of modern realistic literature is one of the manifestations of a striving for truthfulness to life characteristic of this literature, but it is also a reaction against the conventional and lofty style of the baroque literature of the preceding period. Thus the prosaism of style of modern realistic literature is an artistic form, realized against the background of a form in essence opposed to it.[23]

The prosaism of style of the family sagas is of a completely different origin. On the one hand, it is a consequence of the fact that, although these sagas are not simply the recording of oral tradition, they undoubtedly go back in some degree to this tradition. It is not by chance that all the syntactic and lexical features of the language of these sagas are features characteristic of natural and living speech in general, and of oral narration in particular – such features as the predominance of maximally simple syntactic structures connected in an elementary fashion, inconsistency in syntactic linking, irregular alternation of the past tense with the historical present and of direct speech with indirect, predominance of the simplest and most elementary words coupled with highly idiomatic expression, abundance of stereotyped phrases, abundance of demonstrative and personal pronouns and of adverbs of time and place, repetition of the same word in the same sentence. Admittedly, the closeness of the style of family sagas to living speech has also been interpreted as the result of the development of a written tradition, and this paradoxical interpretation has been based on the fact that in the sagas usually considered the earliest – such as *Heiðarvíga saga* and *Fóstbrœðra saga* – the style characteristic of the family sagas is not yet fully developed, while it finds its best expression in *Njáls saga,* generally acknowledged as late. If the family sagas are not a word-for-word recording of oral tradition – and even the supporters of the "free-prose theory" have not claimed this – then it is indeed quite possible that the closeness to the style of oral narration is the result of the development of written literature, something which by no means contradicts the fact that written family sagas had oral sagas as their basis. But complete correspondence between degree of maturity of style and the dating of sagas has, it seems, still not been established. *Egils saga,* for example, is considered comparatively early among family sagas, but no one has ever denied it maturity of style.

On the other hand, the prosaism of style of the family sagas is the consequence of the fact that they are syncretic truth, the product of unconscious authorship. In works representing syncretic truth, the author's creativity was directed, naturally, not so much at content or the transmitted facts *per se*, as at form, i. e. at the way these facts were narrated, at their dramatization and their realization in scenes and dialogues, and the like. But inasmuch as this creativity was unconscious, form too remained unconscious and consequently undistinguished from content. The prosaism of the family sagas is in fact this lack of distinction of form and content, form has minimal independence, there is minimal stylization. Heusler, the scholar who was the best judge of the sagas as art, put it very well: "The language, so to speak, adds nothing to their content. It fits the content without a wrinkle ... The narrator thinks only of the content and wants to render it purely and simply." From this it does not, of course, follow that there is no art in the style of the family sagas. On the contrary, there is in it that supreme art which is possible only in conjunction with unconscious authorship, an art whose essence lies in being imperceptible. Thus, if the prosaism of style of modern realistic literature is a form realized against the background of a form opposed to it, then the prosaism of the family sagas is form not realized as such and not set off from content.

But the essence of the style of the family sagas is most clearly seen if it is compared with the style of the *vísur* (strophes) cited in the sagas as the compositions of various characters mentioned in them. The stylistic difference between these skaldic verses and the prose of the sagas is so enormous that a greater one probably does not exist in world literature. Characteristic for skaldic verse is an extremely mannered form – a very strict meter, a complex pattern of alliteration and internal rhyme, a language differing drastically from that of prose, and abundance of intricate figures (kennings), a completely unnatural word-order – in brief, maximal stylization or maximal differentiation from the way in which language is used in living speech.[24]

A difference is always the sharper, the greater the similarity of background against which the difference stands out. The sharpness of the difference between skaldic *vísur* and saga prose is precisely due to the fact that this difference is only formal. After all, the content of the skaldic verses is, as was pointed out in the preceding chapter, also syncretic truth. Frequently the same thing is reported in them as in the accompanying prose, and this may be due to the fact that they were the source of this prose. But they could also be, it seems, simply its ornamentation. As a rule, certain facts are given in them which represent links in the narration, but by no means anything in any sense more "poetic" than what is imparted in the prose. It cannot by any means be said that the sagas containing many skaldic *vísur* – for example, *Fóstbræðra saga*, *Bjarnar saga*, or *Egils saga* – are in any sense more "poetic" than *Laxdœla saga,* where there are almost none, or *Hrafnkels saga,* where there are none at all. It is also characteristic that in the sagas in which a large role is played by the romantic love of the skalds – as in *Gunnlaugs saga ormstungu* and *Kormáks saga* – much more can be inferred about this love from facts given in the prose than from skaldic verses cited in the saga.

Skaldic verses are, however, distinguished from prose in the sagas not only by form *per se*, but also by the relationship of form to content. While in prose, form is not differentiated from content but is organically fused with it, in skaldic verses form is so mannered and conventional that it is to a considerable degree independent of content. This is manifested most clearly in the fact that it can contradict the content. For example, a beggar may be designated in a skaldic verse by the kenning "distributor of wealth", and a coward or someone who has never been in battle by the kenning "god of battle", not at all ironically, but simply because in the language of skaldic poetry both kennings denote a man in general. The independence of form and content in skaldic verses is also manifested in the fact that one may easily paraphrase them in prose by decoding the kennings and eliminating the unnatural arrangement of words and the other elements of skaldic form, obviously without entailing the slightest loss of content. It is not by chance that commentators on skaldic *vísur* always do exactly that. But to do the same with a saga would be quite impossible. There are no elements external to its content, and it is just in this that the art of the saga lies.

But the most important though least noticeable difference between a saga and skaldic *vísur* lies in the following. As has already been stated, skaldic verses imply the creativity of an author, which, though conscious, is directed only toward form. The relative independence of this form from content is a natural consequence of the limitation of the author's creativity to the sphere of form. The saga, on the other hand, implies the creativity of an author which, though basically directed toward form, is unconscious. Hence the lack of distinction between form and content in the saga, and consequently the possibility of the extension of the creativity of the author to include content. For precisely this reason, it seems, in spite of all the mannerism of skaldic verse, there is less latent fiction in it than in the sagas. This accounts among other things for the fact that skaldic verse originally in a saga has long been acknowledged as a more reliable historical source than the saga itself.

In the family sagas there is absolutely no landscape or description of nature. For this reason, those extremely rare and completely atypical instances when there is something like a portrayal of landscape in a saga are very striking, and have been discussed in the literature about sagas much more than the absence of landscape, which is characteristic of the sagas. Especially felicitous are the famous words of Gunnarr of Hlíðarendi: "How beautiful the hillside is – it has never seemed so beautiful to me, the yellow fields and mowed meadows ... " In fact, the complete absence of landscape is a very important feature of sagas, and it also undoubtedly contributes to apprehension of their art as realism similar to modern realism. Actually, in modern realistic literature landscape portrayal arose as a literary convention, and therefore its absence, for example in the novels of Dostoevsky, may be understood as a liberation from literary convention and an approach to truthfulness to life. The absence of landscape in literature may be understood as close truthfulness to life because such emphatic attention to it as is often found in literature is never observed in real life. In real life attention to landscape is usually reminiscence from literature or painting, and not the immediate reaction of a person to surrounding nature. In literature the perception of nature implied by landscape as a rule characterizes the author and his esthetic tastes, and not at all those of the characters he is depicting against the background of nature. Moreover, inasmuch as a literary landscape always fulfils a definite esthetic function and is somehow bound up with the narrative – by similarity, by contrast, or in some other way – and it is obvious that this connection of landscape with the narrative is introduced by the author and is not present in real life, the literary landscape underlines, as it were, the fact that the narrative is fiction and creative generalization rather than genuine fact. Thus the absence of landscape in modern realistic literature is form perceived as such against the background of a different, more conventionalized form. Obviously, it is a completely different matter in the case of the family sagas. No esthetic perception of nature and no literary landscape existed at all for the people of that time. An esthetic perception of nature implies its opposition to man, with nature as an object external to him. Conversely, the absence of such perception is the manifestation of a unity, not yet lost, of man and nature. Therefore the absence of landscape in the sagas is, of course, not literary form, perceived against the background of a different form, but a definite spiritual content implying limits of human personality different from those which began to predominate when an esthetic perception of nature developed.

The family sagas also have something in common with classical realistic novels in composition. It is characteristic of both, in contrast, for example, to folk tale or courtly romance, that they have an openness of composition, an absence of ready-made traditional plot, that they string together more or less independent episodes, often connected only by common characters. Here too, however, the resemblance between family sagas and realistic novels is purely external. In the latter the openness of composition is, on the one hand, a conscious striving for true-to-life depiction of the multifarious and plotless nature of life, the breadth and openness of the world, i. e. for artistic truth; and on the other hand, it is a reaction against the conventional and closed forms which had earlier been predominant in literature. But in the family sagas the openness of composition is wholly explained by the unconsciousness of authorship and by the fact that the sagas represent syncretic truth. Material not compositionally justified was included either because it was already in the source, or simply because it was accepted as truth. Thus the composition was imposed upon the saga by reality to a far greater extent than is possible in modern literature.

But reality interested the people of that time in one definite aspect – they were interested in events. And an event in Icelandic society was first and foremost a violation of peace – a feud. Therefore, feuds are the basic content of family sagas, and feuds determine their internal logic, their composition. Individual sagas frequently fall quite distinctly into introduction of participants in a conflict, its development, climax, revenge, reconciliation, and aftermath, but this is not of course a compositional device but the natural reflection of the way in which any feud ran its course in reality. The composition of a saga is well organized only to the extent that the content of the saga is drawn from one feud with a small number of participants, i. e. to the extent the feud itself contains a plot, as for example the feud forming the content of *Hrafnkels saga.* But the content of a saga may be a feud in which there are many participants, or several consecutive feuds, as for example in *Eyrbyggja saga.* In such a case, the composition of the saga is much more complex – it may contain several introductions of participants, several climaxes, and so on. Attempts to squeeze such a saga into the Procrustean bed of the scheme outlined above are interesting only as illustrations of how impotent a purely formal analysis is when applied to works representing syncretic truth. Many family sagas break down into more or less independent parts or episodes, as for example *Ljósvetninga saga*, and this too is no compositional device, but is forced upon the saga by its material, i. e. ultimately by reality.

In modern realistic literature, extrinsic elements in a work, such as documents, letters, diaries, and so forth, may be conscious compositional devices. But in the family sagas they are also a consequence of the fact that these sagas are syncretic truth. Everything containing information about a given feud or its participants was included, no matter how the source differed in form or content from the family sagas. Thus the presence of insertions, themselves far removed in style and content from what is considered characteristic of family sagas, is typical of these sagas. A saga may include genealogical lists, legal formulas, fantastic stories of the adventures of Icelanders abroad in the spirit of sagas of olden times, excerpts from kings' sagas, obvious extracts from various other works like the stories of the introduction of Christianity and of the battle of Clontarf in *Njáls saga*, and entire novellas with motifs from fabliaux or courtly romance, like the novella of Spes in *Grettis saga*. The verse in the family sagas, the so-called *lausavísur*, are of course of the same origin. This, however, does not exclude the fact that *lausavísur* in time became a more or less obligatory compositional element in a saga, and were composed especially for it. It is characteristic, however, that usually the less firmly these strophes are connected with the prose, the more obviously they constitute an original element in the saga.

Some of the components of family sagas – the so-called *Íslendinga þættir* ("strands" – they form, so to speak, parts of a saga, as strands form parts of a rope), stories of Icelanders usually in Norway – are commonly printed in modern editions as independent works. Exactly the same kind of *þættir* are also found in the kings' sagas. The meaning of the word *þáttr,* however, like the meaning of the word *saga,* is very vague in Old Icelandic literature. Frequently the same work is called both *saga* and *þáttr,* but other names for parts of a saga are also found (*frásǫgn, æfintýr, hluti*), equally vague. In other words, the *þáttr* was not thought of as a special literary form, and was not clearly distinguished from the saga.[25]

Actually, the unity of an individual family saga is frequently not much greater than the unity of all these sagas taken together. The methods of research into individual family sagas that prevail in modern scholarship lead to an exaggeration of what distinguished them from each other, and to a depreciation of what unites them. And they are united not only by the compositional openness of the individual sagas, but also by the common content of all the sagas – the same society, the same period, the same feuds, and even to some degree the same characters. Indeed, there are characters who not only appear in more than one saga, but who are also treated in exactly the same way in various sagas – for example, Snorri goði, Grettir, and Gestr inn spaki. Moreover, although in individual instances different treatments of the same events are found, for example in *Víga-Glúms saga* and *Reykdæla saga,* or in *Vatnsdæla saga* and *Finnboga saga*), there is no single instance of different attempts in different family sagas to treat the same subject as a whole, as might have happened if events of the saga period were some sort of traditional literary material and did not form the common content of all the family sagas in the aggregate. But if these sagas are regarded as forming, in their totality, a single literary work, then by the scope of their reality they are the greatest work in world literature – a kind of human comedy, in which very many of the Icelanders of the first two centuries of the existence of Icelandic society perform or find mention.[26]

The openness of form of the individual family sagas is also manifested in the fact that they have no titles in the modern sense of the word. In the modern sense, a title is a proper name, invented by the author and forming an organic part of the work. A title in the sagas is something completely different. In oral tradition titles were by no means obligatorily prefixed to sagas, but were used whenever it was necessary to name a certain saga. The formation of a title in the proper sense of the word begins in written tradition at the time when it becomes obligatory to prefix it to the text of a work. It is characteristic, however, that in manuscripts of sagas titles were not always prefixed to the saga but in many instances crop up at the end ("Here I finish the saga of Burned Njáll"; "Here ends the saga of Hœnsa-Þórir": "Here ends the saga of Glúmr"). In oral tradition titles arose, apparently, in exactly the same way as in a certain situation certain word combinations arise, having potentially existed earlier in the language. Just as a house belonging to, let us say, Egill, cannot avoid being called "Egill's house", so a saga telling mostly about Egill cannot help but be called "Egill's saga". The word combination "Egill's saga" existed potentially even before it was used for the first time, and it no more implies conscious authorship than any other word combination in the language, nor is it to any greater extent a proper name – it means only what its component words mean ("saga" and "Egill"), and it does not name or denote something by some conventionalized name.

The family sagas also seem to have in common with realistic novels the fact that they depict private persons in their private lives. The private persons in a realistic novel, however, are by no means the same as the private persons in a family saga. The predominant role of private persons in literary works is one of the greatest achievements of modern times. In medieval literature there were no private persons – the characters were either historical personages, i. e. some definite king or military leader or the like, or the personification of some social station, such as a king in general, a monk in general, or a merchant in general. Thus, in the sagas of olden times (the closest Icelandic analogue to the most widespread medieval genre, the courtly romance) the characters sometimes bear the names of certain historical personages, but more often they are the king's son in general, the viking in general, the *berserkr* in general, and so on. In this way, individualization and generalization are mutually exclusive in medieval literature. If a character is individual, he is a historical personage, or truth in the proper sense of the word, and not a generalization. But if the character is the result of generalization, he is devoid of all individuality – he is a king in general, and so on. In modern literature, on the other hand, an individualization became possible which was at the same time a generalization. Private persons in a realistic novel are a combination of individualization and generalization. The fundamental prerequisites for their appearance in literature are, on the one hand, the possibility of a truth which is recognized as fiction, i. e. artistic truth, and on the other hand, an interest in human personality *per se* – an interest which was unknown to medieval man.

The characters of family sagas differ from the private persons of realistic novels first of all in that they are syncretic truth rather than artistic truth. Consequently, in the minds of the people of that time they were truth in the proper sense of the word, and not generalizations or types.

It is another matter that, owing to the latent fiction present in them, they could in fact be generalizations, if unconscious generalizations. That is why types, after all, are found in the family sagas – ferocious *berserkir,* for example, intriguers and scoundrels sowing discord, women inciting to vengeance, and sorceresses. As a rule, however, they are secondary characters and make up a negligible minority among saga characters. The principal characters, like Egill, Hrafnkell, Njáll, or Snorri goði, are usually more complex, more individualized, and truer to life than any literary types. In a society in which there was no organized state – and consequently no kings, generals, and such personages – the content of works representing syncretic truth naturally had to be the equivalent in Icelandic society of state affairs or the deeds of rulers, i.e., it had to be feuds among the individual members of this society. Thus the characters of the family sagas are not private persons any more than the kings, generals, and other historical personages of medieval literature are; or rather they are at the same time both private and historical persons, a harmonious combination of both, possible only in a society in which there is no division into private matters and state matters, because there is no state.[27]

From the fact that the family sagas are syncretic truth, it follows also that modern conceptions of theme or idea-content are completely inapplicable to them. A character assumed to be truth in the proper sense of the word, rather than artistic generalization or a literary type, can no more be the expression of an idea than a living man in real life can be. It is impossible to be at the same time both a living person and the embodiment of an idea. The latter is possible only if there is an author who embodies it in his work, i. e., is conscious of being an author. But there is no such author either of a living person or of a work representing syncretic truth. It is only in literature representing artistic truth that a character can be the embodiment of an idea. The same also applies to events depicted in a literary work. Modern investigators often read idea-content into certain events described in the family sagas – they find the Christian ethic, for instance, or a protest against the aristocracy. Such a treatment of the sagas implies that they are nothing but parables or fables, i. e., that the events described in them were consciously invented to give expression to a certain idea. But actually the essence of the family sagas lies precisely in the fact that they are something diametrically opposed to parables or fables.

The possibility of idea-content in modern realistic literature is the result of a lengthy development. In the family sagas such a content is found only in embryonic form – in personal sympathies or antipathies and in moral evaluations, frequently, however, inconsistent and contradictory. There is a more highly developed form of idea-content in Christian "miracles" – stories glorifying the power of God and His saints, and abundantly represented in the bishops' sagas and in some of the kings' sagas. The primitiveness of the idea-content of these "miracles" lies in the fact that it is always the same – the glorification of the power of God and His saints. Admittedly, in modern novels, too, the idea-content is sometimes no less primitive, and does not necessarily vary from novel to novel. But the specific character of a work representing artistic truth rather than syncretic truth lies in the fact that the idea-content in it (luckily for the literary specialist?) must be present, even if in the form of a most meager idea, and sometimes against the author's will. For example, it is possible to imagine an author who, although he considers the objectivity of the family sagas as his ideal, nevertheless in his characters invariably embodies ideas with which he sympathizes. But if he is disappointed in these ideas and in ideologies in general, his characters will embody this disappointment and his renunciation of all ideologies. But he will still be equally far from the objectivity of the family sagas, if not even farther, and in comparison with the people told about in them, his characters will seem, as before, only crudely daubed cardboard figures.

An author of our day will naturally be inclined to see in those who wrote the family sagas authors similar to himself. It may seem to him, for example, that they are deliberately concealing their sympathies, views, or knowledge; that this is a conscious artistic device on their part, and that their objectivity is purely a personal, cynical indifference or a coldly mocking attitude to people, expressed in the fates they describe – virtue goes unrewarded, while villainy is unpunished; a good person does evil, and an evil one does good, as frequently happens in the family sagas. The objectivity of these sagas, however, is of course simply the consequence of the fact that they were regarded as truth in the proper sense of the word, rather than as something created by an author. And since a modern author cannot believe that his work is truth in the proper sense of the word, and cannot help being conscious that he is its author, the objectivity of the family sagas is for him absolutely unattainable. The family sagas will always remain the more objective in comparison with any of the most objective realistic literature, the less their authors were conscious of themselves as such in comparison with the authors of this realistic literature.

All this, however, does not contradict the fact that a certain external resemblance is possible between the objectivity of the family sagas and some artistic devices employed in modern realistic literature to create an illusion of objectivity. One of these devices – abundantly represented in the novels of Hemingway – consists in the following. Tragic experiences or events are depicted, not directly, not through the immediate perception of the author, but indirectly, through an especially prosaic and circumstantial perception of a detached observer who apparently does not understand the tragedy of what he observes and only registers the facts. The reader thus finds himself in the position of a first-hand observer of the raw facts of reality which have not been subjected to artistic treatment, and he himself recreates in his imagination what is hidden behind these facts. The prosaic perception of the detached observer serves as a stereoscope, so to speak, imparting in the eyes of the reader a three-dimensional quality to what is depicted. Something similar to this artistic device is detected, for example, in a famous scene in *Laxdœla saga.* The story of the tragic battle in which Kjartan perishes at the hand of Bolli, his best friend who had married Kjartan's fiancée, is prefaced by a conversation between a certain Þorkell and a shepherd-boy. They see Kjartan and his companions approaching the place where Bolli and his men are lying in ambush. The boy suggests running and warning Kjartan of the ambush, but Þorkell dissuades him: "You fool, do you want to bestow life on someone who is doomed to die? To tell the truth, I hope they both do as much harm to each other as they want. I think it will be best if we go off where we will be out of any danger, and can see the fight better and enjoy their play." Then the tragic battle is described, in which Bolli kills Kjartan. It seems, however, that Þorkell's conversation with the shepherd-boy simply underlines the inevitability of death for the person to whom it is fated, as often happens in the family sagas, and does not by any means have the purpose of creating the illusion of objectivity.

In the family sagas, however, it in fact frequently happens that feelings are depicted as if the author has absolutely no interest in them *per se,* but is simply registering their manifestations or consequences along with other facts. The difference from the artistic devices of modern literature is, however, enormous. While in modern literature the person whose indifference of perception serves as a stereoscope is a fiction and the fruit of conscious authorship, in the sagas he is the author himself, unconscious of his authorship. In fact, the sagas do not actually make feelings in themselves the object of description. In this there lies an enormous difference between the sagas and modern realistic literature, particularly the psychological novel. The object of description in the sagas was events that were of interest to the people of that time. Feelings, on the other hand, were described in the saga only to the extent that it was impossible to describe the events without at the same time describing the manifestations or consequences of the feeling, i. e., to the extent the feelings were manifested in the course of the events. Thus the description of feelings is always only the by-product of the description of something else. The objectivity of the description of feelings in the sagas is the result of the fact that they were not the object of description. In this, obviously, lies the similarity of the treatment of feelings in the saga to the modern artistic device described above – what is being described is apparently not the real object of description, and in this way the illusion of objectivity is created.[28]

This may be best illustrated by the manner in which love, in the romantic sense, is depicted in the sagas. The modern reader might often conclude, from the facts reported in a saga, that the person spoken of probably experienced a romantic feeling, although it is evident that the narrator put no such meaning into the facts. The romantic feeling, it seems, did not interest him at all in this instance. Thus in *Egils saga* it is told incidentally how Egill persistently tries to get his brother Þórólfr to take him along to Norway, where Þórólfr is planning to go with his future wife Ásgerðr (who, after Þórólfr's death, marries Egill). Then it is told how, now in Norway, when the time arrived to go to Þórólfr's and Ásgerðr's wedding, Egill suddenly becomes ill and does not go, though he soon gets out of bed and goes on a dangerous journey. Finding himself at a feast at Bárðr's, a steward of King Eiríkr, Egill behaves in an extremely arrogant and provocative manner in the presence of the king and his wife, drinks more beer than anybody else, kills Bárðr in the latter's own house, and, escaping by a miracle, returns home only after Þórólfr had already returned from the wedding. The reader accustomed to finding romantic feelings in literature can easily detect them here too – Egill is passionately in love with Ásgerðr, possibly without realizing it himself; he tries at all costs to go to Norway after her; he suffers from jealousy so that he becomes ill when he is to go to the wedding of Ásgerðr and his brother; in despair he goes on a dangerous journey; he seeks forgetfulness in drink and senselessly risks his life. In the saga, however, the facts cited above are in no way linked with Egill's feelings, and are reported along with many other facts which cannot possibly be linked in any way with his emotions.

Not only did romantic feelings not seem at all worthy of description, but there were also no appropriate words to describe them. For instance, love in the romantic sense was a concept which, at the time when the family sagas were written, had only begun to develop. In the sagas there are three words usually translated as "love" – *kærleikr, elska,* and *ást*. The word *kærleikr* was a new formation, ultimately a borrowing from French, and usually signified the affection or friendship between a king and a member of his guard and the like, rather than a sexual feeling. The comparatively rare word *elska* also usually signified love in the Christian sense, for example, rather than sexual feeling. The word *ást* was used most frequently to denote sexual feeling. Obviously however it did not have the poetic aureole characteristic of the words that denote this emotion in the modern European languages. In the family sagas it is most often used (in the plural) to denote the affection that develops between a man and his wife only after the wedding. "Ástir takask miklar með þeim Þorkatli ok Guðrúnu (Þorkell and Guðrún became very attached to each other)", it is said, for example, in *Laxdœla saga* about Guðrún and her fourth husband. But what remains of romantic feeling if it cannot be described by means of words surrounded by a poetic aureole? Indeed, even in our day, these feelings exist as such only to the extent that they are described in words surrounded by a poetic nimbus. What Pushkin in his famous poem called a "wonderful moment" would, in a description by a moralist rather than a poet, seem simply vulgarity or moral depravity (Anna Kern, to whom Pushkin dedicated his poem, was, after all, the wife of another man).

Even when what is reported in a saga cannot be interpreted otherwise than as the manifestation of a romantic emotion, the conscious object of the description is still not this emotion, but something completely different. In *Ljósvetninga saga* there is the story (in modern editions usually printed as a separate work) of how Þórarinn spaki managed to persuade Guðmundr inn ríki to give his daughter Þórdís in marriage to Sǫrli, Brodd-Helgi's son, as a result of a cunningly conducted conversation. This conversation, reported in detail, and the preceding conversations between Sǫrli and Einarr, Guðmundr's brother, between Einarr and Guðmundr, and between Sǫrli and Þórarinn, form the principal content of the story. But the conversations are preceded by a report of what gave rise to them. Once, when Þórdís went out to her linen, the sun and the wind were from the south, and the weather was fine. She sees a man of large stature riding into the yard. Recognizing the man, she said, "Now it's a great matter, the sunshine and south wind, when Sǫrli rides into the yard!" These words are usually considered the only poetic expression of its kind – of romantic emotion – in the family sagas. But Þórdís's words are cited only because the whole story consists almost entirely of words spoken by somebody, and their poetic quality is probably accidental. There is nowhere else in the story even a hint of romantic feelings, unless, of course, one considers that they are understood inasmuch as Sǫrli is suing for Þórdís's hand. But they hardly seemed understood by the Icelanders of the thirteenth century.

Laxdœla saga is considered a masterpiece because of the manner in which Guðrún's love for Kjartan is depicted. The following paragraphs give everything in which the manifestation of her feelings may be detected.[29]

Kjartan goes to a hot spring in Sælingsdalr. Guðrún, already twice a widow, is usually there. There is talk that they are very well suited to each other. One day Kjartan tells Guðrún that he plans to go to Norway. Guðrún is displeased about this. She asks Kjartan to take her along. But he says this is impossible, and asks her to wait three years. Guðrún says that she cannot promise this. Bolli, Kjartan's fosterbrother and friend, returns from Norway earlier than Kjartan, and Guðrún questions him about Kjartan and learns of the friendship between Kjartan and Ingigerðr, the sister of the Norwegian king. The king, according to Bolli, is prepared to give his sister in marriage to Kjartan. "Guðrún said this was good news. 'Because the woman worthy of Kjartan must be a fine woman.' After this, she broke off the conversation and walked off, blushing deeply." Later that summer Bolli courts her, but she says that she will not marry anyone as long as Kjartan is alive. Later Bolli again proposes. She at first refuses him again, but yielding to her father's persuasions, she finally consents. The betrothal and marriage follow. But the married life of Bolli and Guðrún "was not very harmonious, thanks to Guðrún".

Kjartan returns from Norway and marries Hrefna, and Guðrún upbraids Bolli for lying to her about Kjartan. "It was easy to see that she was unhappy, and many guessed that she deeply grieved for Kjartan, although she hid this." Bolli and Guðrún come to a feast at Óláfr's, Kjartan's father, and Guðrún hears Kjartan say that Hrefna, his wife, will sit in the place of honor. Guðrún, who formerly had always sat in the place of honor in this house, "looked at Kjartan and changed expression, but did not answer". The next day Guðrún asks Hrefna to put on the valuable head-dress that Kjartan had given Hrefna as a wedding gift. As Guðrún apparently knows, this head-dress had been given to Kjartan by the king's sister as a wedding gift for Guðrún. Kjartan does not permit Hrefna to wear the head-dress. The next day Guðrún secretly asks Hrefna to show her the head-dress, which the latter does. Guðrún "unfolded the head-dress and looked at it for a while, but said nothing, either good or bad."

Soon afterwards, Kjartan's sword is missing and so is Hrefna's head-dress. Kjartan accuses Bolli's men of the theft. Guðrún says, "You are stirring up dead coals, Kjartan, and it would be better for them not to smoulder. Even if, as you say, there are people here who are mixed up in the disappearance of the head-dress, I dare say they took what belonged to them. Think whatever you like about what has become of the head-dress, but I don't think it is so bad if Hrefna won't be able to show off in it." Apparently the precious head-dress had been burned by Guðrún's brother at her request.

After this, Kjartan comes with his men to Laugar, where Bolli and Guðrún live, orders all doors to be guarded and no one permitted to come out, forcing all those living there to relieve themselves inside the house for three days. "Guðrún said little about this, but one could understand from her words that hardly anyone took it more to heart than she did." After a while, Kjartan snaps up some land which Bolli and Guðrún had already contracted to buy from the owner. Then Guðrún sharply and persistently eggs Bolli and her brothers to attack Kjartan, and tells Bolli that their conjugal life is over unless he takes part in the attack.

After Kjartan dies at Bolli's hand, Guðrún says, "We have done great things – I have managed to spin yarn for twelve ells of cloth, and you have killed Kjartan." And when Bolli calls this a misfortune, she answers, "I don't call this a misfortune. I thought you were held in more esteem that winter when Kjartan was in Norway, than afterwards, when he trampled on everything, after he had returned to Iceland. But last of all, I'll tell you that more than anything else I am glad that Hrefna will not go to bed laughing tonight." And she thanks Bolli for carrying out her wish. When Guðrún is very old, her son asks her what man she loved most, and she answers evasively, but finally admits, "I was worst to the one whom I loved most."

The account of all this occupies an extremely insignificant place in the total volume of the saga – about five pages out of 248 – and is broken up by the narration of much else relating to the feud under description. Obviously the narrator is not interested in Guðrún's feelings but in the feuding in which Guðrún, among others, takes part. The story concerns Guðrún generally only to the extent that she plays a role in the feud. Nowhere in the saga are her feelings directly alluded to, and those of her words or actions in which her feeling for Kjartan is manifested are reported only in so far as they are indispensable for an understanding of the course of events in the feud. According to the notions of the modern reader, accustomed to the depiction of romantic feelings in novels, these feelings are interesting in themselves, and are even worthy of admiration (in literature, however, not in real life). Such sentimental notions are, however, impossible to detect in the saga. Undoubtedly, admiration was aroused rather by the manner in which Guðrún firmly and pitilessly strives to achieve the execution of vengeance – first on Kjartan for the insults inflicted on her, then on the killers of Bolli, her husband – and the way in which she, determinedly and in defiance of her powerful husband Þorkell, supports Gunnarr Þiðrandabani who is trying to escape vengeance. It is not for nothing that Snorri goði, the great master at attaining his ends in feuds, thinks so highly of her. "Mikill skǫrungr", he says of her – words expressing the highest praise of a person, and implying, above all, energy and determination in carrying out established goals.

Guðrún's emotions seem to be so objectively described because in fact they are not described at all. The reader draws inferences about them in exactly the same way as he might about the emotions of any person in real life. Indeed, in real life too, the emotions of another person are not given by direct observation, but only by their more or less accidental manifestations, which can be variously interpreted. In the saga, just as in real life, a person's emotions can only be guessed at, through their outward manifestations. It is not clear what is concealed behind Guðrún's various words and actions – love for Kjartan, hatred for him, a feeling of pride, injured feminine vanity, a passion for adornment (the precious head-dress), hatred for a rival, a thirst for revenge, or all these feelings together? In the saga, just as in real life, emotions are expressed always, as it were, within very broad limits.

There is not a single family saga in which romantic emotions play the role that they usually play in novels. Even in such sagas as *Gunnlaugs saga ormstungu* and *Kormáks saga,* where the romantic feelings of the hero run throughout the entire saga, by no means everything is subordinated to their description. A great part is taken up, in *Gunnlaugs saga* by the description of his travels to various countries, and in *Kormáks saga* by the description of duels, and in both these sagas the role of romantic feelings is principally to motivate the feuds, which also form their chief content.

In the modern novel the predominant role of romantic emotions is of course due to the increased interest in the human personality, in the private person and his inner world. In novels, love is a means of depicting the personality and its inner world. Admittedly, it would be untrue to assert that love is always the principal content of a novel, since of course novels are possible in which love plays no role at all. But the fact is that love in novels is in general not so much content as form. Therefore, if there is no love in a novel, there is something else permitting the depiction of the personality as lasting in time – travel, for example.

In a certain sense it may be said that feuds play the same role in family sagas as love plays in novels. But a very essential difference between the role of feuds in family sagas and the role of love in novels lies in the fact that feuds really were the most important happenings of that time in Iceland – content dictated by life itself – while romantic emotions have hardly been the most important occurrences in Europe since the novel became predominant in European literature. Moreover, if human sexual life is like an iceberg, whose lower and larger part is hidden beneath the surface, then romantic emotions are only the upper and smaller part of this iceberg, so that even human sexual life is reflected in novels in a very incomplete and consequently false manner. Admittedly, it is known that to some extent reality is transformed under the influence of literature – in the formation of the psyche of modern man, a large role has probably been played by the predominant position long occupied by romantic emotions in novels, although in them they in fact constitute not so much content as form.

What is good and what is evil?

> The impartial observer of the history of morals will acknowledge that the transition from self-help, characteristic of the ancient Germanic peoples, to the state system of punishments was bought at the price of a great loss of moral energy.
>
> *Andreas Heusler*

No matter how objective a description of events may be, it always implies certain ethical notions, from the point of view of which the events are described. Of course, in the family sagas, too, certain ethical ideas are expressed, and they differ substantially from the ideas of a modern man, as would be expected. This difference is apparently greatest in ideas about killing. At the same time, it is probably precisely in ideas about killing that the essence of the ethical conceptions characteristic of the family sagas is most clearly revealed.[30]

Descriptions of slayings in battle are frequent in the family sagas. But the scale of the battles in these sagas, and consequently the scale of losses, are so insignificant in comparison to the scale of battles in present-day warfare, when whole armies are fighting (in the sagas, the battles are essentially no more than duels), and the weapons used in these battles – at most only swords, axes, and spears – are so primitive in comparison to the military equipment of our day, that the killings committed in these fights frequently make no more of an impression on the modern reader than "slayings" committed by a toy soldier in a puppet show.

On the other hand, the modern reader of the sagas cannot fail to be struck by the killings which are committed not in battle or in a fit of passion, but as if they were, both for the slayer and the person describing the slaying, not crimes but completely natural and legal acts. Perhaps, however, the heart of the matter is not in changed ideas about killing, but in changed human nature – perhaps the point is simply that people were more cruel and it was therefore easier for them to kill? It may seem so to the modern reader, when he finds in the family sagas reports of killings such as those cited below.

"He [Kolr] dismounted and waited in the woods until they carried down the timber and Svartr was left alone. Then Kolr ran to Svartr and said, 'You aren't the only one who can chop!' And he planted his ax in his head and struck him a death blow, and then went home and told Hallgerðr of the slaying" (*Njáls saga*). "Eldgrímr wanted to end the conversation with this, and spurred his horse. But when Hrútr saw this, he raised his ax and struck Eldgrímr between the shoulder-blades so hard that the coat of mail burst and the ax went through him and came out through his chest. Eldgrímr fell dead from his horse, as was to be expected. Then Hrútr covered the corpse with earth. This place is now called Eldgrímsholt. Afterwards, Hrútr went to Kambsnes and told Þorleikr what had happened" (*Laxdœla saga*). "Egil dropped the horn, seized his sword and drew it. It was dark in the passage. He ran Bárðr through, so that the point of the sword protruded from his back. Bárðr fell dead, blood gushing from the wound. Ǫlvir also fell, and began to vomit. Egill dashed from the house" (*Egils saga*). "Gautr awoke, jumped up, and started to seize his weapons. But at that instant Þorgeirr struck him with his ax and cleft his shoulder blades. Gautr died from this wound. Þorgeirr went to his tent" (*Fóstbrœðra saga*). "He [Atli] saw no one outside. It was raining hard, and so he did not go out, but put his hands on each side of the door frame and looked around. At that instant Þorbjǫrn appeared before the door and with both hands thrust a spear through Atli" (*Grettis saga*).

„Bjǫrn galloped after them [two outlaws], caught up with them by night, before they could cross the river, and, in short, killed them both. Then he dragged the corpses under a cliff and covered them with stones" (*Bjarnar saga*). "Then he [Hrafnkell] leaped down from his horse and with a blow of his ax killed him [his shepherd Einarr]. After this he went to Aðalból and told what had happened" (*Hrafnkels saga*). Such descriptions of killings are frequent in the family sagas. Of course, the situations vary, but as a rule it is evident from the context that the killing is not committed in a fit of passion. Nevertheless it is described as something completely natural.

In the family sagas young boys sometimes also commit such killings. *Fóstbræðra saga* describes one such committed by one of the heroes when he was fifteen years old. "Þorgeirr was standing some distance from the door. In his right hand he held a spear, point forward, and in his left an ax. Jǫðurr and his men could not see well, because they had come from a lighted room, and Þorgeirr could see better than those who were standing in the doorway. Suddenly Þorgeirr goes up to the door and thrusts his spear through him [Jǫðurr], and the latter falls in the door into the arms of his men. Þorgeirr escaped in the darkness of the night." *Egils saga* tells the story of how the seven-year-old Egill killed another boy who was ten or eleven. "Þórðr gave him [Egill] the ax, which he was holding in his hands . . . They went over to where the boys were playing. Grímr at this time picked up a ball and threw it, and the other boys dashed after it. Then Egill ran to Grímr and drove the ax deep into his head. Then Egill and Þórðr went to their kinsmen." In the same saga, Egill's nine-year-old grandson Grímr kills a twelve-year-old boy. Admittedly, this happens at a time when their adult relatives are fighting among themselves, and Grímr himself is seriously wounded. And in *Heiðarvíga saga* Snorri goði eggs on his young fosterson Þórðr, nicknamed "cat" (*kausi*), to attack the nine-year-old son of his enemy: "Does the cat see the mouse? The young should strike at the young!"

In the family sagas, killing not in battle or in a fit of passion is committed or, if they cannot do it themselves, encouraged and approved by even the most peaceable men. Thus, when Njáll – undoubtedly one of the most peaceable heroes of the family sagas – learns from his sons that they have killed Sigmundr and Skjǫldr, he says, "May your hands be blessed!" And learning of the killing of Gunnarr, he tells the sons of Sigfús that several men will have to be killed to avenge Gunnarr, killing which is in fact carried out by Njáll's son Skarpheðinn and Gunnarr's son Hǫgni. Later he instructs his sons how to behave so that they will be sufficiently insulted by Þráinn in the eyes of others, and will thus have the right to kill him. Finally, Njáll's refusal to leave the burning house and save his own life is motivated by the thought that he will not himself be able to kill those whom he considers it his duty to kill – the slayers of his sons – and life therefore has no meaning for him.

Nevertheless, to conclude from all this that people were then more cruel than now would be completely false. To begin with, these killings were as a rule, as is always evident from the broad context, not ends in themselves but the fulfilling of a moral obligation, a duty. Admittedly, the content of duty was in this case usually some form of revenge – for a kinsman, for oneself, or (in the case of the slaying of Einarr by Hrafnkell) for one's horse – i. e. not at all what a modern man considers his moral duty. But from this it does not by any means follow that duty imposed itself on a man any less strongly then than in our own day. From what is told in the sagas of how the duty of vengeance was carried out, how unhesitatingly any risk was taken and any sacrifice made in order to carry it out, it is evident that the power of this duty was greater then than nowadays. And the fact that the killings were not committed in fits of passion is by no means evidence of cruelty, but only of the power with which the duty of vengeance imposed itself on a man.

The killings in the family sagas are not evidence of cruelty, moreover, because they are never accompanied by torture of the victim or by violation of his corpse. Decapitation of the victim, which is sometimes mentioned in the family sagas, symbolized victory over an enemy, and was not intended as a violation of the corpse. In fact, in the language of the sagas there is no word for "cruelty" or "cruel" in the sense of the deliberate infliction of torture. Tortures are mentioned only in the kings' sagas – they were employed by the Norwegian kings to persuade heathens of the truth of the Christian religion. In the family sagas torture is unknown. In general, although killing could happen outside battles, as in the above examples, it was still always somehow analogous to battle – as a rule, only men were killed, not women and children; the killing was usually committed during the daytime; the blow was usually struck openly, not from behind or from an ambush; and it was customary for the killer to report to someone at once what had happened. It is not by chance that the Old Icelandic word meaning "killing" (*víg*) also means "battle".

The fact remains, however, that killings are mentioned rather frequently in the family sagas, and to the modern reader it may seem that this is evidence of an abnormal interest in killing – of cruelty. But such a conclusion would also be completely erroneous. A modern man always involuntarily ascribes to people of other periods whatever is characteristic of himself. In our day a morbid interest in murders has made them obligatory in the most popular of modern literary genres – the mystery novel. In the family sagas, killings are mentioned not at all because there was a morbid or abnormal interest in them, but simply because peaceful life was not considered a theme for story-telling. Only violations of the peace, i. e. feuds, were considered such a theme, and the feuds were naturally accompanied by killings. Besides, the family sagas are syncretic truth, so that the killings in them are not literary fiction, as in mystery novels, but facts imposed upon the sagas by reality. Precisely, however, because these sagas are not about peaceful life, but about violations of the peace, they reflect reality in a very one-sided manner. The modern reader may receive the impression that during the "saga age" – the period during which the events described in the family sagas took place – killings occurred especially often. But if one considers that these sagas preserve information about most of the killings that took place in the country during the course of about a hundred years (the killings took place, after all, during feuds, and the family sagas tell about most of the feuds that occurred during the "saga age" – only information about some feuds seems to have been lost, but they were hardly numerous), one must conclude that not so many killings in fact took place during the "saga age". The number of killings *per capita* over a hundred years in a modern society, especially if killings in wars are taken into account – and there are no grounds for not including them – would, of course, prove immeasurably greater.

The idea, widespread in Icelandic studies, that the so-called "age of the Sturlungs" – the period when the family sagas were beginning to be written – was especially cruel, seems also to be a misunderstanding. This period seems cruel chiefly because *Sturlunga saga*, the principal source of our information about the period, is taken for "history" in the modern sense of the word. In fact, however, this saga, too, reflects reality very one-sidedly – it too tells only of feuds. A no less false idea of our time would probably be formed by people of the future, if no literature were to be preserved other than reports of military actions and court records of criminal cases. Admittedly, the feuds of the "age of the Sturlungs" in Iceland took on a somewhat different character from those of the "saga age", connected with increasing economic inequality and increasing influence of the church. The difference between *Sturlunga saga* and the family sagas, however, is still more due to the fact that the former was written soon after the events occurred, and the events were consequently less subjected to epic stylization.[31]

But if it is not true that in the "saga age", just as in the "age of the Sturlungs", people were more cruel than in our day, we are left with the assumption that the ideas of those times concerning killing were different from ours. Was killing considered something generally bad, worthy of condemnation? Obviously not. Very often it was obviously regarded as a heroic deed, the fulfilling of the highest duty, something which elevated a man in the eyes of others and was worthy of praise. It is not by chance that glorification of killing and boasting about killing occupy such a large place in skaldic poetry. But then, was killing perhaps considered something generally good and worthy of praise? Also obviously not. In many cases it was clearly regarded as an act deserving condemnation and discreditable to the one who committed it.

A modern man invariably wants to find general concepts among people of past ages, where there were only more specific ones. From evidence from the Old Icelandic language it is obvious that the people who spoke that language had no concept for "killing in general". There were only concepts for killings of specific character. As has already been said, the Old Icelandic word *víg* denoted not only "killing", but also "fight", "battle". In a number of cases, these two meanings were combined, for example in compound words of the type *víg(a)hugr* ("warlike mood", "desire to kill"). The word *víg*, however, did not connote every killing, but only a killing in battle or an overt killing; as a legal term it connoted a killing which the perpetrator immediately reported not further away than the third house, and for which he could thus be prosecuted by law and could, if the other side agreed, redeem himself by paying wergild. If, on the other hand, the perpetrator of the killing did not report it properly, it was no longer *víg*, but *morð*, and its perpetrator was considered outside the law. The word *morð* also denoted the killing of a sleeping person, a killing carried out at night, and in general any killing carried out in an improper fashion. In poetry, however, the word *morð* was used as a synonym of the word *víg*. In *Gísla saga* still another variety of killing is mentioned – *launvíg,* something between *víg* and *morð*. The killer in this case did not report what he had done, but he left his weapon in the wound. If *morð* was always something deserving condemnation, *víg* was sometimes something bad (for example, if the slaying was unprovoked and the slayer moreover refused to pay wergild), and sometimes something good (if the killing was in fulfilment of the duty of vengeance). A practice which was also not considered reprehensible in pre-Christian times was the so-called "bearing out" (*útburðr*) – the abandonment of a new-born child in the open air if the parents had no means of feeding it, a custom widespread among the peoples of the world and still known in China, for example, in the twentieth century. But the law permitting *útburðr* was revoked soon after Christianity became the official religion in Iceland. In the family sagas the custom of *útburðr* is mentioned several times, but usually with condemnation.

Thus, as is clear from linguistic evidence, there was no conception of "killing in general" nor of killing being always evil. But consequently there also did not exist that contradiction which became inevitable with the rise of the organized state, when it became the custom, on the one hand, to condemn – in essence hypocritically – any killing, and on the other hand, to justify killings necessary for the protection of the state from its external and internal enemies, i. e. killings on a much greater scale and of much greater cruelty than those occurring in a society where there was no conception that killing was always evil. The English "killing" (as well as the corresponding words in other modern European languages) always implies this conception, so that in so translating the word *víg* in the family sagas we are ascribing our own modern conceptions in this area to the saga heroes. Killing in the modern sense would rather translate what in the sagas is denoted by the word *morð*.

As has already been said, killings in the family sagas are usually committed because of the duty of revenge. So the conceptions of killing characteristic for these sagas were obviously defined by the role played by the duty of vengeance in the life of society. In works devoted to ethics in the family sagas, much is said of "honor" as the basis of this duty, "honor" (in writings by German scholars it is often also called "Germanic honor") being understood sometimes as something external to the man – as some blessing received from others – sometimes as something internal, a kind of self-respect, and sometimes as something both external and internal. But it is characteristic that in Old Icelandic there is no equivalent of the modern word "honor", though there are a number of words which, with more or less straining, could be translated by this word, such as *sœmð, virðing, sómi, metnaðr, vegr, frami, metorð, vegsemð, heiðr, mæti, hǫfuðburðr, drengskapr.* It seems that in all cases where a modern word signifying something in the sphere of the mind corresponds to several words or to numerous words in an ancient language (such is also the case, for example, with "glory", "soul", and "luck"), the difference between the modern and ancient ideas is so great that it is useless to try to express the ancient ideas by means of the modern words.

The people of the society in which the duty of vengeance played such an important role were not, of course, aware of what constituted the basis of this duty. The enormous power with which it imposed itself on people was obviously due to the fact that it was not engendered by a system of concepts (such as "honor" or "duty") inculcated by training, but arose directly from social conditions; as the result of the social experience of many centuries it became, as it were, an automatic reaction. In a society in which there were no state institutions to ensure the security of its individual members – no police, prisons, courts, and the like – there was nobody to protect the individual from his enemies. He had to protect himself with the help of his kinsmen and friends, i.e., he had to resort to vengeance, particularly its most effective form – killing. In such a society property damage or other forms of damage inflicted upon the individual and maiming or killing as a rule incurred vengeance. With the rise of state institutions, vengeance, or self-help, yielded to a state system of punishments. The enemy became the criminal.

But in Iceland in the thirteenth century state institutions still existed only in embryo. In the "saga age" there was not even a trace of them. Self-help prevailed, and its principal form was revenge – most often killing. It has been calculated that in the feuds mentioned in the family sagas there are 297 acts of vengeance, for the most part bloody (i. e. killings); 104 cases of peaceful arbitration without litigation; and only 119 lawsuits, nine of which however were violently broken off, while 60 ended in peaceable arbitration. But even the lawsuits in the sagas were – as Heusler, the foremost investigator of them, aptly put it – only a "stylized vengeance". The lawsuit was not conducted by a judge or a representative of the state – there could be no such representative – but by the litigants themselves. Therefore the outcome of the litigation was usually determined by the practical relationship of the litigants' forces at the *þing,* rather than by the degree of validity of the suit. It was no accident that litigation at the *þing* sometimes turned into a real battle, as happened during the famous suit at the *alþingi* described in *Njáls saga.* Finally, carrying out the sentence was the responsibility of the plaintiff himself, or of anyone who for some reason undertook it; otherwise the sentence remained an empty word. Thus, self-help was the rule even in a lawsuit. The social conditions in which the duty of vengeance was developed still prevailed in Iceland in the "saga age", and had still not died out in the period when the family sagas were written.

In order for blood revenge to be an effective form of self-help, it had to be a duty, i. e., it had to be carried out independently of a man's feelings, his sympathies or antipathies, his love or hate, his sense of injury or anger, even his feelings of justice. For this reason, killing from the duty of revenge is not at all the same as revenge in the modern sense of the word. In carrying out the duty of revenge, a man risked without hesitation his own life or that of his relatives, accomplished long and difficult journeys, and displayed enormous self-restraint in biding his time for a suitable opportunity, sometimes many years. Many instances of such delayed revenge are described in the family sagas. To accomplish revenge quickly or to carry it out in a fit of passion was considered a bad performance of duty. On the contrary, the longer a man waited for an opportunity to carry out blood revenge and the more self-restraint he thus exhibited – and thereby the less impassioned he was in its commitment – the better the duty was performed. An Icelandic proverb, known from *Grettis saga,* says, "Only a slave avenges immediately, and only a coward – never." In other words, only a man with no feeling of duty carries out revenge in a fit of passion. When passion is absent, the fulfilment of duty appears, as it were, in a pure form.

Once slaying in revenge came to be carried out independently of the slayer's feelings, or even counter to them, blood revenge could be directed, not at the offender himself, but at his kinsman or a member of his household. The selection of the object of the blood revenge was not determined by his participation in the infliction of the damage, but by his importance in the eyes of others, by how dangerous he might be in the future, or simply by chance. Thus blood revenge could be directed against a man toward whom the avenger could have no feeling of injury, anger, or hatred. In this connection, Hrafnkell's slaying of Eyvindr in *Hrafnkels saga* is typical. Eyvindr's brother Sámr humiliated the powerful Hrafnkell, brought about his outlawry and forced him to leave his possessions and settle in another district. But in revenge Hrafnkell did not kill Sámr, but his brother Eyvindr, who had just returned to Iceland after an absence of seven years and who had no connection with what had happened to Hrafnkell; and when Sámr fell into Hrafnkell's hands, Hrafnkell spared him.

Thus, if a killing in a feud was revenge for another killing, the man slain in revenge might not be the original killer himself, but his kinsman or adherent. It was important that the total number of those slain in a feud be equal on both sides. Therefore, if the feud ended in arbitration, a calculation was made – the killing of so-and-so balanced the killing of so-and-so, and somebody's wound balanced somebody else's wound. A difference in the number of killed or wounded could be compensated by wergild. A curious example of how strongly the need was felt to balance losses in a feud is contained in *Eyrbyggja saga.* There was a battle between Þorbrandr's sons and Steinþórr and his men, and one of Þorbrandr's sons was killed. No one on Steinþórr's side was killed, only his younger brother Bergþórr was seriously wounded and left in a boat-house. Another of Steinþórr's brothers, Þormóðr, was married to Þorgerðr, Þorbrandr's daughter and thus the sister of her husband's enemies. According to the saga. "They say that Þorgerðr did not want to lie in the same bed with Þormóðr, her husband, that evening. But at that time a man came down from the boat-house and said that Bergþórr had just died. After he had said this, Þorgerðr went to bed with her husband, and nothing is said of any discord between husband and wife after this."

Inasmuch as blood revenge was a duty, it was natural for it to seem a good thing and a heroic feat. It was the best satisfaction of an injured party and the greatest honor to a slain man. Revenge killings were celebrated in verse, and they form one of the principal themes of the sagas. But it was also natural that, because of this, the mastery of weapons was compulsory and universal for men, and bellicosity, courage, and consequently the ability to kill were highly esteemed. Therefore, although the notion did not exist that killing in general was a good thing and a heroic deed, sometimes, it seems, a murder might be committed only to prove one's ability to kill. In *Fóstbræðra saga,* Þorgeirr Hávarsson heroically kills his father's slayer (see p. 98) and carries out a number of other heroic killings, but once he decapitates a shepherd only because the latter was standing so that his neck was convenient for the blow. And in *Flóamanna saga* the boys agree among themselves that they will not accept as a playmate a boy who has not killed some animal. Þorgils Þórðarson, then five years old, lies awake at night and tries to think what to do to ensure that he is not left out of the games any more. "He got up, took a bridle, went out of the house, and caught sight of the horse Illingr in the yard. He went there, took the horse, and led him to a house. Then he took a spear, went up to the horse, and thrust the spear into his stomach, and the horse fell dead. And Þorgils went to bed." The idea that there is something heroic in killing, even if it is unprovoked and reprehensible, finds expression even in the language of the sagas. "People will call this both a great feat (*stórvirki*) and an evil one (*illvirki*)" says Flosi, the chief of the "burners", of the burning of Njáll. Every killing was a "great feat" (*stórvirki*) or a "great undertaking" (*stórræði*). On the other hand, the idea that there is something heroic in killing frequently makes itself felt in our day too, and not only in boys' games, but it usually takes on a more hypocritical form.

Very much has been written concerning the degree to which heathendom and Christianity are reflected in the family sagas. In recent times it has been customary to assert that, although the cult of Christianity is reflected very sparingly in them, basically they express the Christian world-view, the ideas of a believing Christian, and so on. Formerly, on the other hand, it was customary to assert that, although pagan cults are reflected very sparingly in these sagas, basically they express a pagan world-view, pagan morals, pagan spirit, and so on. But it seems that in both attitudes the role of any official cult in the formation of the human psyche is greatly exaggerated. Official cults form strata, owing to various historical conditions, on the deep subconscious ideas that are the basis of human behavior and human perception of the world, but these cults by no means necessarily express these ideas. Admittedly, in written literature arising under the conditions of a highly developed organized state an official cult with its dogmas, mythology and phraseology usually more or less obscures these deeply rooted ideas. One of the huge advantages of the family sagas over all the rest of medieval literature lies in the fact that official cults, pagan as well as Christian, are very sparingly reflected in them. So the family sagas constitute exceptionally favorable material for the study of conceptions more deeply rooted in the human psyche than cult ideals and dogmas.[32]

What is taken for a Christian trait in the family sagas is usually "Christian" only in the sense that it continued to exist after the introduction of Christianity. Moreover, when it is assumed that the family sagas must express the Christian world-view, the conversion to Christianity is apparently imagined, perhaps unconsciously, in the same way as Christian missionaries imagined it – as an automatic and instantaneous transformation into a qualitatively new man with a qualitatively different consciousness – once people became Christians, their psyche also became Christian. This is evidently the way Christianization is imagined. Such faith in the wonder-working nature of conversion to a new religion is understandable in missionaries, of course, but it seems strange in modern scholars. For them, it seems, the consciousness of a heathen differs from the consciousness of a Christian of the same period immeasurably more than the medieval consciousness differs from the consciousness of a modern man. In other words, in these scholars' conception of the human mind, the confessional point of view, rather than the historical one, is predominant. Actually, the replacement of one official religion by another – especially if, as was the case in Iceland, such a change was not accompanied by any material changes in the social structure – could not also lead to significant changes in human consciousness. This is especially evident in the case of the conceptions of killing reflected in the family sagas, works written no less than two centuries after the acceptance of Christianity in Iceland. These conceptions were the direct result of the social conditions existing before, as well as after, the conversion to Christianity. It is therefore natural that it did not lead to any significant changes in these conceptions. For the Christian believer as for the pagan believer, killing in revenge was a heroic deed, and failure to kill was a disgrace.

But those who declared that the family sagas for the most part express pagan conceptions also exaggerated the role of religion. These conceptions are also "pagan" as a rule only in the sense that they also existed during pagan times. If, however, they were preserved after the conversion – and sometimes even until modern times, like the notions for example about the "living dead" reflected both in sagas and modern Icelandic folktales – they are obviously rooted more deeply in the human psyche than any official cult ideals.

But all this does not, of course, exclude the possibility that ideas more deeply rooted in the human psyche than cult ideals and dogmas could to some degree be adapted to an official cult. Thus in the pagan age, the conceptions of killing described above could be linked with the cult of Óðinn, as the god of war and death to whom the slain were dedicated. In the Christian period these conceptions could be linked with the cult of the Christian God. In the family sagas it is repeatedly reported that a person intending to kill out of revenge turned to the Christian God and received help from Him. For example, the following is told in *Njáls saga.* The blind Ámundi approaches Lýtingr, who had killed Ámundi's father, with a demand for wergild, but Lýtingr refuses. Then Ámundi appeals to God and at once regains his sight. "God be praised, my Lord! Now I see what He wants," he says, and kills Lýtingr with an ax-blow on the head, after which he again becomes blind. In the same saga, Hildigunnr adjures Flosi "by all the miracles of Christ" to avenge the slaying of her husband

Hǫskuldr. In *Hávarðar saga,* the aging and infirm Hávarðr makes a vow to become Christian if he succeeds in killing the powerful Þorbjǫrn, who has killed Hávarðr's son. And Hávarðr is able to kill him on the spot, when Þorbjǫrn slips and the rock with which he had intended to kill Hávarðr falls on his own chest. Subsequently Hávarðr goes to Norway and is baptized. And in *Fóstbrœðra saga* the Christian God is glorified for helping the fifteen-year-old Þorgeirr carry out blood revenge for the slaying of his father (see p. 98): "Everyone who heard this news thought it surprising that a youth had killed such a warlike chieftain and such a valiant warrior as Jǫðurr. But it was not surprising, for the Creator of the world had created and placed in Þorgeirr's breast such a fearless and firm heart that he feared nothing and was as fearless in all trials as a lion. And since everything good is created by God, courage, too, is created by Him and placed in the breasts of brave men, along with the freedom to do what they want, good or evil. For Christ made Christians His sons and not His slaves, and He rewards everybody according to his deserts."

Such an attitude toward blood revenge is, however, not typical of the official Christian ideology. Indeed, the commandment "Thou shalt not kill" is considered one of its cornerstones. But was the Christian "Thou shalt not kill" anything more humane than the conceptions of killing which prevailed in the family sagas? Under the conditions of the Christianization of medieval Scandinavia – when state power in the person of king and church took into its own hands the rights and obligations which had formerly been the prerogative of the individual member of society, in other words, when the self-help that had predominated yielded to the state system of punishment – the Christian "Thou shalt not kill" was, of course, the greatest hypocrisy.

The right to punish and, in particular, to kill shifted from the individual to the state, to be used by the latter on a far greater scale than had been possible for the individual. But now killing was committed, not in revenge for oneself or one's relatives and friends, but by a higher order or by the order of God, the ideal prototype of state power. Each man thus became a potential hired killer or executioner. Thus, the hypocritical attitude to killing was legalized, since at the same time the commandment "Thou shalt not kill" was being preached, i. e., killing in general was condemned, although the true sense of this commandment was "Thou shalt not kill thine enemy, but thou shalt kill the enemies of the king and of God". With the introduction of Christianity, torture came into use. People were tortured and executed for refusing baptism, i. e., killing in the name of an idea became possible, something formerly unknown and something which made killing possible on a previously unheard-of scale. Thus, the abdication of his rights and obligations to the state or to a punishing and rewarding God, with His hell and paradise, was a restriction of the independence and freedom of the individual, a diminishing of his moral responsibility, and a blow to his self-respect and dignity, and thereby a prerequisite for the development in him of an inferiority complex.

In works concerning the family sagas it is customary to regard any evidence of humaneness or peaceableness in these sagas as the result of Christian influence. This is evidently based on the conception of Christianity as a humane and pacific ideology. This conception would perhaps be understandable in reference to the sentimental Christianity which became widespread in Europe relatively recently – Christianity without belief in the torment of sinners in hell, without intolerance, without the cult of self-torture and other forms of sadism and masochism long characteristic of Christianity. In reference to medieval Christianity this conception is absolutely false.

With regard to peaceableness it is obvious that this trait had to be valued even in a society in which self-help prevailed and open killing was legal. In such a society people would soon have annihilated each other, if there had not existed the idea that unprovoked killing is bad, i. e., if people had not valued peaceableness. "Harvest and peace" was the customary request made of the gods during a feast in a pagan temple. Positive appraisals of people in the family sagas are most frequently "well liked", "having many friends" (*vinsœll*), and "calm", "restrained" (*vel stilltr*), i.e. peaceable; while the negative ones were "not liked" (*óvinsœll*), "overbearing", "intractable" (*ódœll, óvæginn*), "tyrant", "bully" (*ójafnaðarmaðr, óeirðarmaðr, vígamaðr*), i.e. not peaceable. Especially peace-loving heroes of the family sagas – such as Áskell in *Reykdœla saga,* Ingimundr and his son Þorsteinn in *Vatnsdœla saga,* Gunnarr and Njáll in *Njáls saga* – have recently been explained as Christian reinterpretations of pagan heroes, as an attempt to make pagan heroes into forerunners of Christianity. But in this way the writers of the family sagas are credited with the sentimental conception of the Christian religion which became current in literature only in the nineteenth century.

It is no coincidence that both the chief heralds of Christianity in western Scandinavia – the Norwegian kings Óláfr Tryggvason and Óláfr Haraldsson (Saint Olaf) – began their careers as vikings, and in the sagas about them a large part is taken up by their warlike exploits. The fact that Christianity was by no means humane and peaceable is obvious from the numerous and often very detailed accounts of its introduction into Iceland and Norway. The sagas in which these accounts are preserved were written by faithful Christians, so that, although not everything in them, of course, is historically exact, there are no grounds whatsoever for doubting that the moral essence of Christianity, as it still was in the period when the sagas were being written, is transmitted correctly in them.

For example, in the saga about King Óláfr Tryggvason, written by the monk Oddr Snorrason around 1190 for the glorification of Óláfr as an Icelandic national hero (in his reign Christianity was introduced into Iceland), much is told about pagans agreeing to be baptized, not because they realized the moral superiority of the Christian religion but because the king compelled them to accept it, through tortures, executions, and intimidation with hell's torments, or by otherwise convincing them that the Christian God was stronger than the pagan gods or simply that he, Óláfr, was stronger than the pagans. Allied with Emperor Otto, Óláfr Tryggvason fought against the Danish king and the Norwegian jarl. "Everywhere they went," reports the saga, "they ordered the people to be baptized, and then they would not rob them. Most of the people, for their salvation, accepted baptism, and those who did not want to accept it were killed." When Sigurðr Hlǫðvisson, jarl of the Orkneys, refused to be baptized in spite of the king's intimidations with "the torments of hell, eternal fire and freezing, and many other terrible tortures", the king seized the jarl's young son and threatened to cut off his head before the jarl's eyes if the latter did not accept baptism. Only then "did the jarl agree both to being baptized and to making peace with the king. The jarl and all his people were baptized." The inhabitants of the island of Mostr were persuaded of the superiority of Christianity only when three of their orators, who had been commissioned to defend paganism, suddenly lost the gift of speech – one had a fit of coughing, another began to stutter, and the third was attacked by hoarseness. In Trondheim, the king gathered the local aristocracy at a feast, then proposed that they all either be sacrificed to the pagan gods, i. e. killed, or be baptized. "One or the other," he said, "be baptized or be sent to your gods." They all agreed to be baptized. "That way is better for all of us," graciously said the king.

In the second year of his reign, the king "declared all those outside the law who were skilled in magic or followed the old belief, especially those men and women whom the Norwegians call sorcerers and sorceresses, and ordered that they be killed like outlaws or murderers." Once, having gathered all the sorcerers and sorceresses under the pretext of a farewell feast before their departure by ship from Norway, he gave orders to burn the house where the feast was in progress, "and a dreadful wailing and howling of women, and men arose," as the saga reports.

Hróaldr of the island of Goðey persisted in paganism, and the king presented him with the choice – abandon paganism or die – and threatened him with cruel tortures. Hróaldr preferred death. "Seeing that Hróaldr persisted in his belief, the king ordered him to be hanged on a high gallows, and thus he died." Haukr and Sigurðr, two Norwegians just arrived from England who did not want to be baptized, were put into irons at the king's orders. But on the third night they managed to escape to Hárekr, a powerful Hálogaland chieftain who was persisting in paganism. The king offered Hárekr the control of two *fylki* (districts) if he would accept Christianity, but Hárekr refused even three. When, however, the king offered him four *fylki*, he agreed. Then Haukr and Sigurðr, too, had to accept baptism. Another Hálogaland chieftain, Eyvindr kinnrifa, who did not surrender to the persuasions of the king and did not agree to being baptized even for five *fylki*, had a basin of live coals placed on his stomach by order of the king. Dying, Eyvindr explained that he could not be baptized because he was not a man, but an evil spirit that had been lured into his mother's womb by sorcery. Thus the evil spirit died with burning coals on his stomach.

Pagans who had gathered in the temple in Frosta in Trondheim were persuaded by the king of the superiority of the Christian religion when he chopped up their idol of Þórr, while his men killed their leader Járnskeggi. The powerful Hróaldr í Moldafirði, who was persisting in his paganism and with the help of sorcery would not permit anyone to approach his dwelling, was taken captive by the king, and when Hróaldr still refused to be baptized, the king ordered him to be killed. Once at a *þing* at which the king was preaching Christianity, when a pagan began eloquently to object, the king ordered him to be seized and had a snake forced into his mouth. The snake crawled into his mouth when a piece of red-hot iron was tied to it and crawled out of his belly with the heart of the eloquent pagan in its mouth. "And seeing this, all the pagans were very frightened," reports the saga. But nowhere in it, and in fact nowhere in Old Icelandic sagas is anything related which might be evidence that Christianity impressed the pagans with the superiority of its morals. The pagan gods, in whose existence the author of the saga obviously believed (both Óðinn and Þórr appeared, according to this saga, to Óláfr Tryggvason in human form), were in his view simply less powerful than the Christian God.

Snorri Sturluson in *Heimskringla* further tells how Óláfr Tryggvason tried to persuade Rauðr inn rammi, a wealthy landowner from Goðey, of the superiority of Christianity over paganism. The king with his fleet attacked Rauðr at night, slaughtered many of his men, and captured Rauðr and offered him baptism, promising to release him and let him keep his property. "But Rauðr fiercely refused the offer, saying that he would never believe in Christ, and blaspheming terribly." Then the king became angry, and ordered that Rauðr be tied to a log, a tube placed in his mouth, and a live snake forced into his throat. Rauðr still did not understand the superiority of Christianity and died, gnawed by the snake. "King Óláfr there seized," Snorri goes on, "much gold and silver and other property, weapons and various treasures, and all the people who were with Rauðr he ordered to be killed or tortured."

In the so-called *Legendary Óláfs saga helga,* written for the glorification of this herald of Christianity and preserved in a manuscript of the middle of the thirteenth century, a great deal is told of battles in which he killed many people and amassed much wealth by robbery, and also of how he compelled the acceptance of baptism under the threat of death. *Óláfs saga helga* in *Heimskringla* also tells of this, but in greater detail – for instance, "if some did not want to abandon heathenism, he [Saint Olaf] banished some from the country, ordered that others have their hands and feet chopped off or their eyes put out, others he had hanged or put to death by the ax, so that no one who did not want to serve God was left unpunished".

In Iceland there was no royal power, no institution which needed the support of the Christian church and which could use it for subjugating the people. For this reason Christianity was introduced into Iceland without the threat of torture and death. Even in Iceland, however, the missionaries did not stop short of killing, as is seen in *Kristni saga.* Þorvaldr Koðránsson, one of the first Christians in Iceland, killed three men because of *níð* (defamatory verse) composed about him and the German bishop Friðrekr. Admittedly, in the *níð* it was said (and this was indeed extremely insulting in those times) that the bishop had born nine children by Þorvaldr. The German priest Þangbrandr, who was later a missionary in Iceland, once killed a man in a duel – the rascal wanted to take a beautiful Irish slave-girl away from the priest. Subsequently Þangbrandr went on a viking crusade against the heathens and took a great quantity of booty. King Óláfr Tryggvason sent him to Iceland to preach Christianity; there Þangbrandr and his followers killed first the skald Vertrliði, then Þorvaldr inn veili, because of *níð*, and in a fight with some men from whom Þangbrandr and his followers had bought food by force, nine more men were killed. In *Njáls saga* it is further reported that Þangbrandr killed a certain Þorkell in a duel – the scoundrel had dared to come out against the creed that Þangbrandr was preaching.

As is obvious from *Kristni saga*, the Icelanders did not by any means accept Christianity because they found higher morals in it; they accepted it because the missionaries succeeded in convincing them of the power of the Christian God. Koðrán Eilífsson was baptized because the sacrificial stone, in which, as he thought, his guardian spirit lived, burst when Bishop Friðrekr uttered a prayer over it. Þorkell krafla and numerous others permitted themselves to be baptized after a fire, blessed by the same bishop, burned some ferocious *berserkir* who did not fear fire. Gestr Oddleifsson and his friends let themselves be baptized after a fire, blessed by þangbrandr, burned the feet of another ferocious *berserkr* who did not fear fire. And so it went on. It was not by chance that Þorgeirr goði in his famous speech at the *alþingi* based the necessity of accepting Christianity in Iceland only on political motives, and did not say a single word about the moral superiority of Christianity.

The moral essence of Christianity for the people of that time was naturally not all humaneness and peaceableness (these became the attributes of Christianity only in the sentimental and anti-historical fantasies of modern scholars), but the generous reward of all pious believers, i. e. all those worshipping the Christian God, and the cruel punishment of all sinners, i. e. all those not worshipping Him – all pagans in the first place. The reward for worshipping the Christian God seemed real, particularly because of the belief in miracles, zealously spread by the church. And the reality of punishment for not worshipping Him was provided by the activity of those heralds of Christianity who subjected the heathens to execution and torture, and by the belief in the terrors of hell, also zealously spread by the church. As is stated in the *Elucidarius*, a scholastic treatise which enjoyed enormous popularity in the Middle Ages and which was translated into Icelandic apparently as early as the end of the twelfth century, the greater part of humanity will end up in hell, including many children older than three years, as well as all who were not baptized; the greatest enjoyment for those saved from hell will be to observe the condemned writhing in eternal torment in hell.

In this moral principle of reward and punishment from above, there is obviously nothing humane and peaceable. And it was a great regression in comparison to the moral principle of self-help. The principle of reward and punishment is widely represented in the bishops' sagas, and not infrequently in the kings' sagas; in the family sagas it is almost totally absent. This is obviously due to the fact that, although Christianity was introduced into Iceland at the turn of the eleventh century, the Christian God could not, owing to the absence of state institutions in Iceland, enjoy there the same authority that He enjoyed, for example, in Norway, where His cult was propagated by the king himself. After all, a change in *what* people believed did not signify a change in *how* people believed – belief in God was for the people of that time not so much belief in His existence (in the minds of the people of that time, it seems, the pagan gods existed side by side with the Christian God) as belief in His power.

Nevertheless, Christian belief in miracles is represented here and there, even in the family sagas. It may appear that the transition from belief in sorcery, condemned by Christianity – and this belief is very widely represented in the family sagas – to Christian belief in miracles was also a change only in what they believed, not in how they believed. But this is not the case.[33]

In the accounts of sorcery abundantly represented in the family sagas frequently nothing occurs that could not take place in reality. For example, in *Kormáks saga* the following story is told: Kormákr struck a whale with a spear, and the whale sank, but people thought that the whale had eyes like those of the old woman Þorveig. It was known that she was a sorceress and consequently could change herself into a whale; and at that very time Þorveig became very ill and died. In *Vatnsdœla saga* it is reported that a shepherd saw Gróa, who had the reputation of being a sorceress, come out of her house, go around it counter to the sun and look at the nearby mountain. She waved a small bundle containing a large gold ring, and said, "Let go what is ready to go." Then she went into the house and closed the door. The landslide which soon after buried the house and everybody in it, including the sorceress, is regarded in the saga as having been evoked by her actions. Completely real facts – bad weather, illness, death, shipwreck, cattle plague, landslide, failure in love, and the like – are frequently considered the result of sorcery in the family sagas. In Old Icelandic there are even special words for bad weather and for illness caused by sorcery (*gerningaveðr* and *gerningasótt*). But very often nothing fantastic actually occurs as the result of the acts of sorcerers and sorceresses. Thus a belief in sorcery did not prevent an objectively accurate perception of the facts of reality themselves, and was manifested only in fantastic explanations of the causal relationships between these facts.

But it is possible, after all, that much of what in our day seems a correct explanation of causal relationships will appear equally fantastic to future generations.

On the other hand, the belief in miracles propagated by the church usually implied a fantastic conception of the very facts of reality – in Christian miracles a blind person suddenly regains his sight, a cripple is instantaneously cured of his affliction, a wound heals without a trace, a corpse gives out a wonderful aroma, and a dead person returns to life. In other words, something occurs which could not occur in reality.

But a no less essential difference between sorcery and Christian miracles lies in the fact that sorcery implied knowledge, skill and technique, at times quite complex. It was necessary to utter certain words, sing something in a special manner, know how to use runes, be able to make certain movements with the hands or with a special instrument such as a magic staff or kerchief, make a certain sacrifice, build a special structure, and observe certain conditions, at times very difficult ones. It is no accident that learned men in folk tradition often have the reputation of being sorcerers, like Sæmundr inn fróði in the Icelandic folk tradition. For its own time, sorcery was the analogue of modern scientific experiment. Techniques of sorcery seem fantastic to the modern man. But there is frequently an element of fantasy in the techniques of scientific experiment too. In this sense the scientific experiment (may the scientific experimenters forgive the author) is often a kind of sorcery. But in order to produce a Christian miracle – as follows from the stories of miracles in the sagas – no skill, no knowledge, and no technique were necessary. It was only necessary to appeal to God or one of His representatives on earth, such as a saint. The Christian miracle was only the reward for slavish adoration, or punishment for the refusal of such adoration.

Can time be stable and what is death?

> There is indeed really no question here of past and present in the same uncompromising sense as with us, who always move with faces half buried in a dark cloud, and a clammy feeling about the neck. Time lay spread out about those people of old.
>
> *Vilhelm Grønbech*

A passion for travelling is more and more taking possession of humanity. More and more, travelling is becoming a necessity for man – travelling in time as well as in space. Formerly, in turning to the past, a man actually remained in the present – the differences of past ages from the present did not interest him, and he did not notice these differences. Now man more and more strives to grasp past ages in their differences from the present, and thereby to escape, in a way, from the present into the past. But such a voyage in time, no matter what, will always remain an illusion – man remains in the same time, and time remains the same for him. A voyage in time that is not illusory is, however, possible – by the apprehension of temporal concepts different from ours, by grasping another perception of time.

Greatly generalizing, it may be said that the difference between the conceptions of time in the family sagas and our modern ones lies in the greater unity of the former – the absence of any split, contradiction, or break.[34]

If events described in a literary work are recognized as artistic generalization, or fiction, they are by this very fact taken out of the framework of real, historical time or that general stream of time in which all events that actually took place in the past are thought of. Events of any "novel of contemporary life", though described in the past tense, are not at all thought of as being in the historical past, but rather in some conventionalized, fictitious, "artistic" or "literary" time. This literary time is in a way parallel to real, historical time, and is itself an artistic generalization or fiction. It is precisely for this reason that such novels are recognized as describing the present. Literary time is the creation of the author of a literary work – he depicts the flow of this time, places events in it, and arranges it in accordance with the general intent of his work. In fact, even the meaning of grammatical forms of the past tense is different in literary works from their meaning in real life or in historical works. Such forms of the past tense assign the action to a fictitious past with the purpose of generalizing something which in reality is not the past at all.

The family sagas imply the absence of a break between time in real life – real, historical time – and time in literature – unreal, fictitious time. Everything described in these sagas was syncretic truth, i. e., it was regarded as having actually happened in the past and thereby it was assigned to real, historical time. The solidity of this assignment to real, historical time was ensured in many ways in the family sagas – people mentioned in them were links in genealogical chains leading ultimately to the real present; all events in the sagas were attached to concrete localities in Iceland; these events were ultimately attached to important historical landmarks such as the settlement of Iceland, the conversion, or the reign of a certain Norwegian king; events and persons mentioned in the sagas were connected by cross references. In fact, Old Icelandic sagas, on the whole, never tell of events removed from the framework of the general historical flow of time. Conventionalized time, parallel to real time, does not occur in them at all. A saga of contemporary life is as unthinkable as a saga of the future. Even in the so-called sagas of olden times – obviously fantastic works – the action is not so much removed from the framework of historical time as moved to its periphery: the events described in these sagas are regarded as having occurred very remotely in time, and often very remotely in space as well.

In a modern novel – whether a novel of contemporary life, or a historical novel of the life of any past age, or even a fantastic novel about life in the future – events may be treated in principle in the same manner, i. e. with greater or less dramatic quality, realism, and the like, since the action in all varieties of the novel is conceived of as occurring in a conventionalized literary time, parallel to historical time. It is characteristic of Old Icelandic sagas, on the other hand, that a given treatment of the narrative is completely conditioned by the time of the occurrence of the matter narrated. From the viewpoint of modern literary study, *Sturlunga saga* and other sagas telling of events of the twelfth and thirteenth centuries, the family sagas (the sagas of events of the tenth and eleventh centuries), and the sagas of olden times (the sagas of events prior to the tenth century) are three distinct genres. Each of these three saga varieties is characterized by a specific manner – roughly speaking, documentary and naturalistic, dramatic and realistic, and adventurous and fantastic, respectively. But from the viewpoint of the thirteenth-century Icelander, all these works were simply "sagas". The modern terms for these three saga varieties originated later. The only differing factor seems to have been the time in which the events described in the sagas took place. Thus time, though indivisible, was not, as it were, uniform throughout its span.

The lack of uniformity of time was manifested chiefly in the fact that events described in a saga were the less subjected to the requirements of verisimilitude, the more remote they were from the present. As was said in greater detail in the chapter "What is truth?" (p. 38), this is probably ultimately bound up with the fact that in oral tradition information is not so well preserved about things remoter from the present. But in the sagas this is undoubtedly a definite conception of time. It is not by chance that Snorri Sturluson, telling in his *Heimskringla* of events of the period from the ninth to the twelfth centuries, obviously strives to remain within the bounds of verisimilitude, avoiding ecclesiastical miracles and omitting much of the implausible that was in his sources. On the other hand, in the mythological *Ynglinga saga*, in which more ancient events are narrated, and in *Gylfaginning*, in which the action also takes place on the periphery of historical time, Snorri opens the door wide for the supernatural. Admittedly, he seems to incline toward a euhemeristic treatment of pagan mythology, i. e. a treatment of the pagan gods as deified human beings, but the inconsistency of his euhemerism is probably due to the fact that he himself was by no means free from the idea that peripheral time was a time when the supernatural was possible. The predominance of the supernatural and the fantastic makes possible the timelessness of a narrative – the absence of any localization in time. For this reason the fairy tale is in principle timeless. Fairy-tale timelessness is, it seems, the embryonic form of conventionalized literary time.

The time of the action of the family sagas has something in common with the so-called "epic ages" (ages to which the action in epic poetry is assigned). It, too, is strictly localized in real, historical time – the "saga age", as is well known, is usually regarded as the period approximately from 930 to 1030. But the "saga age" differs essentially from the "epic ages" in that it is not isolated and does not occupy an insular position, but is connected with both the following age and the preceding one – the age of the sagas of olden times. This connection consists, on the one hand, in abundant genealogies going beyond the limits of the "saga age" in both directions, and on the other hand, in the existence of works which combine peculiarities of two successive saga varieties – family sagas and sagas of olden times, or family sagas and sagas of a later age. Admittedly, a certain isolation of the "saga age" may be detected in the fact that there is a break of almost a hundred years between the age told of in the family sagas (it ended about 1030) and the age told of in the sagas of events closer to the time of writing, which begins no earlier than 1100 or a little later. It is possible that this break is not accidental, but is evidence of the existence of a certain tendency to transform the "saga age" into a kind of "epic age".

Real historical time is characterized by a single direction, an irreversibility. For fictional time, on the other hand, singleness of direction is not obligatory, and its fictional nature is most evident when this is violated – when the narrative turns back, or anticipates events and then turns back. The "narrated time" is cut up into pieces, so to speak, and these are arranged in an arbitrary order in accordance with certain artistic aims. In the family sagas no transposition of time ever takes place. This, of course, is due to the fact that time in them was regarded as real, historical time. On the other hand, a parallel account of events in two different places is possible in the family sagas, if this does not violate the singleness of direction of time, and in some of the sagas this is widely employed for dramatic effect. Singleness of direction of time is also not violated by prophecies, portents and the like, since these are elements of the present.

The modern consciousness is characterized by a split between "objective" time – that unending continuum of time existing in nature independent of events occurring in it and independent of its perception in the consciousness of the individual – and "subjective", "psychological", or "internal" time – that time inherent in the experience of the individual, oriented in its flow in relation to his consciousness, time which may be felt as flowing slowly, imperceptibly, quickly, fleetingly, and so on, and seems finite, moving to its end – the death of the individual. Every modern man is conscious, on the one hand, of what Newton called "absolute, true, and mathematical time", which as he says, "by its nature flows in and for itself without regard to any outward object". But on the other hand, it is also characteristic of modern man that he constantly feels behind him the swift approach of "time's winged chariot", in the words of Andrew Marvell, the seventeenth-century English poet. The absence of a split between conventionalized and real time is an important characteristic of the psychology of the family sagas. But it is less striking than the absence of a split between "objective" and "subjective" time.

A subjective apprehension of time is never manifested in the family sagas, either in the point of view of the author or in that ascribed by the author to the characters. In fact, such an apprehension of time could not, of course, be manifested in these works, either in the author's viewpoint – since there generally is none – or in what is ascribed to the characters of the sagas, since their emotions are never analyzed or described. A rudimentary manifestation of a subjective apprehension of time might perhaps only be detected in the expression "langt þykki mér" ("I am bored"; literally, "it seems long to me") in the last *vísa* of Egill Skallagrímsson. But Egill's verses are not the family sagas.

It would be a mistake, however, to conclude that since there is no "subjective" time in the family sagas, time in them is therefore "objective", i. e. the same as the time our modern science operates with. The fact is that the conception of time as an even and uninterrupted stream, completely independent of what occurs in it, is also absent in the sagas. Such a conception developed gradually and probably chiefly as the result of the spread of time reckoning by means of units which are not also phenomena of nature. A man who is accustomed to looking at the hand of a clock or watch and to reckoning time by such abstract units as hours, minutes, and seconds must have a different conception of time from a man who, like the Icelander of old, was unacquainted with clocks, and reckoned time only in such units as night, day, winter, and summer – units which are also phenomena of nature. Time was less abstracted from natural phenomena or other events taking place in it.

In modern editions of the family sagas it is customary to analyze the "chronology of the saga" and to reduce the dates established by such an analysis to a chronological table (for example: Gunnlaugr's birth 984; Gunnlaugr's going to Borg 999; Gunnlaugr's voyage to Norway 1002). Some items in such tables are, of course, simply guesswork or assumption. But it is possible, nonetheless, to compile such tables, since one finds in the family sagas not only numerous instances of dating of the type "once in the morning", "once in the evening", "the next morning", "the following day", "in a short time", "in the spring", "that same autumn", and "in a few winters" – dating which reflects, as it were, the eternal aspect of time – but also sometimes dating of the type "the summer when Eiríkr rauði went to Greenland", "at the time when King Haraldr hárfagri gained power in Norway", and "fourteen winters before the conversion". But in the family sagas, of course, no instances of dating of the type "in the year 984" or "at the beginning of the tenth century" are ever found. The superimposing of an abstract chronological scale on events related is absolutely alien to the family sagas. Thus a scholarly analysis – in this case the compilation of a chronological table of events – as often happens, not only fails to help us understand the psychology of the work being analyzed, but on the contrary obscures it. In fact, to superimpose a chronological scale on events in a family saga matches illustrating such a saga with a picture of its hero in a nylon zippered jacket, sitting behind the wheel of a racing car.

The fact is that in the family sagas time is not an even and uninterrupted stream. It forms a unity with events, and is inseparably linked with them and registers on the consciousness only in so far as they take place, and exists only in them. This is evident from the fact that in the family sagas, only events are generally related, and not even all events but only those connected with some feud; and neither nature, nor everyday life, nor the feelings of the characters, nor anything at all that existed independently of events, is ever described. There are in the family sagas no scenes beginning an action. Such introductory scenes are usual in novels. But such scenes imply a static description, made at a certain moment of the action, and are therefore impossible in the sagas. It is characteristic that the appearance of the characters in a saga is frequently described for the first time just before an important event in their lives – such as a battle or duel. A man's appearance is, in a way, part of an event. It is characteristic also that if such things as dress are described in a saga, it is not, as a rule, the typical that is described, but the atypical, something which deviates from the usual and is in itself a kind of event.

If no events occur, the saga sometimes reports this in such stereotyped expressions as "things were calm for a while", "it was quiet for a year", "it was quiet for two winters, so that there is nothing to tell", or "nothing happened to tell about, during their stay there", but most often nothing at all is said – it is as if time ceases to exist, and resumes only with the next event. For example, in *Njáls saga* after Njáll takes Hǫskuldr to foster, time ceases to exist and begins again in the next section of the same chapter (94), when Hǫskuldr is already grown up, and events take place in which he plays an important role.

Static descriptions, which are absent in the family sagas, imply a perception of time more abstract than that characteristic of these sagas. Such descriptions imply an ability to make a mental cross section of the stream of time at any one of its moments, regardless of whether any event is taking place at this moment, and to imagine what would be observed at the moment of this cross section – in other words, the ability to realize that not only events take place, but that something is always taking place, however gradual and imperceptible. It is precisely this ability, it seems, which is the basis for what is called the historical point of view. In the family sagas this ability is totally absent. Indeed, the historical viewpoint does not always come easy, even to a modern man. Thus, changes which do not come about as the result of events and in sudden leaps are in fact not seen by those modern philologists for whom "artistic quality", "learned quality", "authorship", and the like are eternal and immutable entities.

Everything that did not change as a result of events or sudden leaps, but gradually and imperceptibly, such as economic or legal conditions, family life, and so on – in other words, everything that was only in the background of events – is reflected in the sagas as if somehow telescoped in time and anachronistically, so that in the description of events of the "saga age", conditions or features of everyday life of a later age show through. In a historical novel a certain age is consciously reproduced. Admittedly, the psychology of the characters in it is as a rule contemporary with its writing. In a saga everything is telescoped – everyday life, customs, law, morals, and psychology. A saga is similar to a geological formation in which the deposits of different ages are pressed together, and it differs from a historical novel in the same way as a modern architectural monument, built in the style of a certain past age, differs from an ancient monument, reconstructed many times.

In the kings' sagas time is more abstracted from the events taking place in it than in the family sagas. The reign of a king forms the core, hence their name. But the reign of a king comprises not only events; it is also the flow of time. Therefore in the kings' sagas, in contrast, to the family sagas, time is severed from events, is objectivized, and begins to exist by itself. Hence the appearance in the kings' sagas of a chronological scale superimposed on events, the beginning of the year-by-year account of events, and the attaching of events to a year in the reign of a king. A chronological scale superimposed on events also appears in the bishops' sagas. Some events are included in a saga only because they are united by one year's cross section. The internal bond of events characteristic of the family sagas yields to the bond of simultaneity. Even, however, in the Old Icelandic annals or yearly chronicles – works whose essence is provided by a chronological scale – there are found names for winters or summers which individualize them, not by number but by what happened in them: *kynjavetr* ("winter of wonders"), *skriðnavetr* ("winter of landslides"), *fellivetr* ("winter of loss of livestock"), *manntapavetr* ("winter of human deaths"), *frostvetr* ("winter of frosts"), and *býsnasumar* ("summer of portents").

But the psychology of the family sagas differs from the psychology of modern man in nothing so much as in the apprehension of the past and the future in relation to the present. For a modern man only the present is real, not the past or future. His interest in the past is not the result of an organic bond with it but is either a purely theoretical interest resulting from the development of the historical viewpoint, or, in the case of romantic idealization of the past, an escape – a flight from the real present into the unreal past. But as a rule even yesterday's events are no longer interesting to a modern man. Who reads old newspapers? Out of the enormous number of events taking place in the world, his attention is attracted by only a few, and not for long even by them. Indeed, only what is happening in the present actually exists. What happened in the past or will happen in the future does not exist. Man seems to be isolated in the present. His position in time is insecure. An abyss separates the present from the past and from the future. Man is poised on a steep slope from which he may at any moment slide into the abyss. The instability of time and the insecurity of man's position in time became a favorite theme of poets as early as the Renaissance.

It is impossible to detect any traces of such a conception of time in the family sagas. A firm organic bond with the past and a consciousness of one's unity with it are revealed in them first of all by the enormous space occupied by information about the past – information which of itself could offer nothing esthetically significant, like names, genealogies, and data concerning kinship. In our day, such information would interest only the historian, the narrow specialist on the particular period, but not the ordinary reader unconnected with the scholarly study of history. But this type of information was not only always included in the written sagas – and consequently was read, listened to, copied and recopied – but it was repeated and listened to many times in the oral tradition (it could unquestionably never have been preserved from the "saga age" except in oral tradition). In other words, this information enjoyed wide popularity in the society. Everything that happened in the past was of interest.

The firm bond with the past in the psychology of the family sagas was caused primarily by the fact that the interval separating the past from the present was perceived as a concrete chain of generations, rather than as a lapse of abstract time. It is for just this reason that genealogies play such an important role in the family sagas. This firm bond with the past was, however, also caused by the strength of family continuity and by the firmness and importance of the bonds of kinship. Indeed, the chief subject matter of the family sagas is made up of feuds, and into the feuds were drawn numerous persons, mutually bound by various ties of kinship, and the role of each participant was determined by these ties. Thus the individual in the family sagas exists not in a chronological framework but in a genealogical one. Moreover, since the motive power of a feud in the family sagas is always the duty of vengeance, going from kinsman to kinsman, any feud was a relay race not only from the past to the present, but also from the present to the future. Faced with a violent death, a man worried about whether sufficient wergild would be paid for him. "I want to ask you," says Atli, for example, in *Njáls saga*, "that, if I am killed, it is not the price of a slave that is paid for me." Assurance that he would be avenged reconciled a man to death. "I am gladdened by the thought," says Skarpheðinn in the same saga, "that if you escape, brother-in-law, you will avenge us." In this way a firm bond was created, not only with the past but also with the future – a kind of super-temporality of the consciousness.

But the firmness of the bond with the future in the psychology of the family sagas also has other roots – in the belief in fate; this belief in turn implies a certain conception of time.[35]

It is universally acknowledged that belief in fate plays an enormous role in the family sagas. Much has been written concerning this belief, and a little has even been established. For instance, it has long since been established that, manifesting itself in prophetic dreams, portents, presentiments and prophecies, it plays an important role in the composition of the sagas, forming the connecting thread of the narrative. The assumption that belief in fate in the family sagas is simply a "compositional device" is, however, absurd, in particular because in a number of instances its presence obviously plays no compositional role. But belief in fate is not the "author's philosophy", either, since it appears in all the family sagas to a greater or lesser degree (most of all in *Vatnsdœla saga, Njáls saga, Víga-Glúms saga, Laxdœla saga,* and *Gunnlaugs saga ormstungu*). And it has never crossed anyone's mind that the family sagas were written by one author. Belief in fate is, of course, not at all "idea-content" in the usual sense. It is only what existed in real life and was therefore expressed in literature faithfully reflecting life. And in life, as in the sagas, it was expressed in sayings and proverbs such as "you cannot escape fate" (there are numerous such proverbs in the family sagas and very many in the Icelandic language), in the idea of dreams foretelling the future, in accounts of prophetic men and women and people with second sight, and the fulfilment of omens, presentiments, auguries and prophecies.

Belief in fate obviously contradicts Christian teaching. For this reason, the attempt to explain it by Christian influence is nothing more than a curiosity. But to consider it the heritage of a pagan cult, as has usually been done until now, is also scarcely correct – this belief is also represented among peoples with other official cults, for example in the classical world and among the Islamic peoples. It is therefore more probable that the roots of a belief in fate lie in some deep peculiarities of the mind, most likely in a conception of the stability of time, in what may be called the "spatialization of time" or the "spatial metaphor of time" – the conception that the near and the remote in time, i. e. the present and the future are equally stable and real, just as the near and the remote in space are equally stable and real. Indeed, belief in fate – the belief that the future, the remote in time, cannot be changed but may be known through prophecies or seen in dreams – implies that the future in a way possesses a kind of reality and exists in the present, exactly as the remote in space exists and possesses reality. Such a conception of the future is one of the manifestations of the close bond between temporal and spatial concepts characteristic of people in that early period.

The spatial metaphor occurs very frequently in designations of time. For example, in English the spatial preposition "before" is used metaphorically in a temporal meaning (cf. "before evening", and the like). It is possible that such a linguistic metaphor is ultimately due to a certain conception of time, its "spatialization". But in relation to the psychology of the family sagas, it is not a question of a linguistic phenomenon, of course, but of a definite cast of mind. A man about to be killed in an approaching battle already bears the real mark of this. In a way his future death already exists. It is designated by the word *feigð* (which does not lend itself to translation into modern languages). A future unfortunate fate (*ógæfa*, also a word untranslatable into modern languages) already sets its mark on a man in the present. In a way it already exists. Thus one may perceive from the external appearance of a man that he is a man with a future unfortunate fate (*ógæfumaðr, ógæfusamligr maðr, eigi gæfumaðr*). An impending misfortune may be seen with one's own eyes. It makes itself known in ominous portents or dreams. It already exists in the present. A woman, touching a man about to go into battle, can feel with her hands the places where his wounds will be. They already possess reality. A weapon which will slay an enemy in an approaching battle makes this known by its ringing, since the fatal blow to be inflicted by this weapon is already something real. Such conceptions follow from what is recounted in the family sagas.

Bound up with belief in fate – and thereby also with certain conceptions of time – is, apparently, the characteristic attitude toward death which appears constantly in the family sagas. In these sagas there is never a description of fear of death. But instances of the absence of such fear are constantly recounted (it is a question, as a rule, of a violent death in battle or as a result of an attack, since a natural death from sickness or old age is usually not described at all, and only occasionally mentioned: after all, such a death is not an event). The last words of a man faced with inevitable death usually bear a purely matter-of-fact character or contain an objective announcement of some sort. If a man dying of a fatal wound composes a *vísa,* like Gísli in *Gísla saga* or the skald Þormóðr in *Fóstbræðra saga,* this *vísa* – like, incidentally, any skaldic *vísa* – is strictly formalistic and also contains an objective report of some sort of facts. These accounts of a man dying often contain completely true-to-life details, and no doubt in their time seemed as a whole completely true to life, i. e., they reflected reality, even if they were fiction.

On the other hand, on us today the accounts in the family sagas of a man dying may produce a comical effect, so different is the attitude of modern man toward death. *Grettis saga,* for example, tells how Atli, Grettir's brother, was killed. Þorbjǫrn, Atli's enemy, knocks at the door, and Atli, not knowing who is knocking, comes to the entrance. “He saw no one outside. It was raining hard, and so he did not go out, but put his hands on each side of the doorframe and looked around. At that instant Þorbjǫrn appeared before the door and with both hands thrust a spear through Atli. ‘They are now in style, these broad spearheads,’ said Atli, receiving the blow, and fell prone on the threshold.” In *Njáls saga* it is told that when Kolr Egilsson’s leg was cut off at the thigh in a battle, he said, “I paid for not having protected myself with my shield.” The account continues, “And he stood for a time on the other leg, looking at the stump. Then Kolskeggr said, ‘There is nothing to look at. That’s the way it is – the leg is off.’ And Kolr fell dead to the ground.” In the same saga, the Norwegian Þorgrímr, on whom Gunnarr had inflicted a fatal spear wound from the window, upon being asked if Gunnarr was at home, answered, “Find out yourselves. I only know that his spear is at home.” And he fell dead to the ground. Of course, to a certain extent such depictions of death reflect the heroic ideal of a warrior’s behavior rather than reality. But this heroic ideal had itself a certain grounding in reality. Moreover, it is characteristic that the death of the peaceable and by no means warrior-like Njáll is, in fact, depicted in the same way. His last words, uttered in the blazing house, is a statement on how he will be lying in the bed (along with his grandson and his wife), so that their bones will be easier to find in the charred ruins.

Accounts of instances of disdain for death are found not only in the family sagas, but also in sagas telling of events in Iceland in the twelfth and thirteenth centuries. For example, in *Sturlunga saga* (more precisely, in *Íslendinga saga* by Sturla Þórðarson) it is told that after the battle of Ǫrlygsstaðir, when several of the prisoners were executed, Þórir jǫkull, before being executed by the man whose brother he had killed, composed a skaldic *vísa* in which he expressed his fearlessness in the face of death (it ends *Ást hafðir þú meyja, eitt sinn skal hverr deyja* – "You have had the love of maids, and one dies only once"). In *Sturlunga saga* there are several more detailed and dry reports of such executions and displays of disdain for death by the condemned. In *Hákonar saga gamla,* Sturla Þórðarson tells of the death of Duke Skúli, pretender to the Norwegian throne: "When the duke saw that they [his enemies] were going to burn the cloister, he told his men to go out. They went to the door. The duke also went out, holding his shield before his face. He said, 'Don't strike me in the face, since that is not done with rulers.' And they killed him and all who came out with him."

It is customary to explain this disdain for death in the pagan period by the influence of the heroic ideals of paganism, and in the Christian period by the Christian thirst for martyrdom. It is, however, much more probable that the basis of this attitude toward death is formed by conceptions more deeply rooted in the human mind than any official cult ideals, either pagan or Christian. Disdain for death can hardly be explained by notions of life beyond the grave, characteristic of various cults. As is known, pagan ideas of life after death (if one judges by the traces of them in the family sagas, for example) were extremely unclear and contradictory, possibly as a result of the fact that the notions of different ages were superimposed on one another. After death, a man continued to exist either as a disembodied soul (named and imagined in various ways), or – and this is found most often – as a completely corporeal "living corpse"; and his abode was Óðinn's palace Valhǫll, or Hel, the kingdom of the dead (it is not clear where it was situated), or inside a mountain in which all his dead ancestors lived, or, if he had drowned, in the abode of Rán the sea goddess, or simply in his grave, or finally in one of his descendants in whom he continued to live. The Christian idea of life after death is, however, also very contradictory – on the one hand, it is a man's soul only that lives on after death, while on the other hand, sinners in hell experience completely physical torments. In the family sagas there are very few traces of the Christian teaching on life after death, and the fear of death which would take possession of people if they believed in the Christian teaching of the torments of hell is completely absent. Judging by Icelandic folk tales reflecting the ideas of a much later age, the notion of the "living dead" remained prevalent in Iceland, i. e. the notion that a dead man lives on in his grave in corporeal form, seeing and hearing, eating and drinking, experiencing anger, happiness, fear and the like – in a word, possessing all the characteristics and faculties of the living.[36]

There is only one thing common to all these notions of life after death – for the individual, time does not end with death; it possesses stability. And this stability of time is most distinct in the notion of the "living dead" – the notion that a man, after death, remains essentially the same as he had been in life. The belief in life after death is not the cause but the consequence of the idea of the stability of time. It is not any notions of life after death which determine a man's attitude toward death, but his ideas of time. If time is indivisible and stable and does not end with death, then death is not really so fearful. It is much more fearful for a man if an abyss lies between time in nature and time in the individual experience – what was and what will be do not exist, the present is the only reality, and it is only an instant, and the consciousness is isolated in it, and time has no stability.

Is it worthwhile to return from the other world?

Every dream comes true in the way in which it is interpreted.

Icelandic proverb

The contents of this chapter are somewhat unusual for a work in which are set forth the results of a scholarly investigation. The fact is that the material for it was provided by the utterances of an apparition which appeared one April night in a room in the Saga Hotel in Reykjavík.

On the night when the conversation with the apparition took place, the author of this book had returned to the Saga Hotel from an Icelandic home where those present, as is customary in Iceland, were telling of ghosts they had seen in their lifetimes. In order not to lag behind the others, the author also told a ghost story. But, since he himself had never before chanced to see ghosts, in his story he himself appeared in the role of such a ghost. He had supposedly died back in Leningrad, as the story had it, and only his ghost had come to Reykjavík. The story was heard out, as is customary in Iceland, with complete trust. For that reason, returning that night to the Saga Hotel, the author was not firmly convinced that he was a living man and not a ghost. Entering his room on the sixth floor and turning off the radio, which had just broadcast the latest weather report, the author stood at the window. It took up an entire wall, and from it one could see the city, the ocean, and the sky, lit by the sunset. They say that Reykjavík has the most beautiful sunsets of any city in the world. Probably they are right. But Reykjavík's sunset is not only very beautiful. Admiring it, one involuntarily asks oneself whether it is not a delusion . . .

Suddenly the author distinctly felt that someone had appeared behind his back. Turning away from the window, he saw, in the depths of the room, near the wall, a strange figure with sad eyes in a pale face and a grey beard; he was dressed in a long, wide garment. The stranger was the first to break the silence. Unfortunately, there is no tape recording of everything that he said that night. At first the stranger's speech was difficult to understand. He was obviously speaking Icelandic. But he did not pronounce the Icelandic words in the way in which, according to the opinion of historians of the Icelandic language, they must have been pronounced earlier. What it was that made his language not immediately understandable was not easily determined. But is seems that he had various peculiarities in the articulation of the vowels. It is quite possible that these were articulatory peculiarities characteristic of the phonetics of ghosts in general.

It turned out that the stranger's name was Þorleifr. He immediately also gave his father's name, and those of his grandfather and great-grandfather and great-great-grandfather and so on, tracing his family back to one of the first settlers of Iceland, and he began to trace it back still further, but suddenly gestured sadly and his eyes filled with tears. He said it did not matter – nobody in Iceland remembers these people, and if they were to hear of them, they would not remember their names. Indeed, I succeeded in remembering only that among Þorleifr's ancestors, there were a certain Þórðr, somebody named Þórir, either a Þorkell or a Þorgrímr, some woman named Hallbera, and that Þorleifr was separated from his ancestor, one of the first settlers of Iceland, by eight or nine generations. Consequently, he had lived not later than the first half of the thirteenth century.

It further turned out that Þorleifr had been wandering around Iceland since autumn. As could be understood from his story, he had been disturbed in his grave during the laying of a pipe from some hot spring, and since then had not been able to find rest. He had tried to look up descendants or kinsmen among present-day Icelanders, but without success. Nobody he talked to could name among his ancestors a single one of Þorleifr's contemporaries. Moreover, nobody at all knew all his own ancestors by name. Some unblushingly admitted that they did not even know the name of their great-grandfather. Nobody knew even all his own contemporaries by name. Many did not even know the names of people who lived in the next house. Þorleifr was completely without kin in present-day Iceland, and was more alone than he had been in the grave. There he had at least had the bones of his kinsmen nearby. But, as one could understand from his words, he was crying not only because he felt himself without kin and solitary, but also because he was sorry for the people he met – they, while still living, were just as solitary and deprived of kin as he, who had lain seven hundred years in the earth. Since, however, he knew nothing of the generations that had lived after him, he obviously could not imagine how much time had passed since his death. This time, apparently, did not exist at all for him.

But Þorleifr, as it turned out, was sorry for the people he met not only because they seemed solitary and without kin, but also because at the same time they lived, as it seemed to him, in monstrous overcrowding. Indeed, in Iceland now there is just as much space as there was in his time. But people invariably build their houses on one small promontory – he evidently had in mind the promontory on which Reykjavík is situated (where, as is known, almost half the entire population of Iceland lives) – while the greater part of the country remains just as deserted as it was at the time of the first settlers. He had formerly thought that only sheep could be reconciled to such overcrowding, when, driven from summer pastures into sheepfolds, they meekly wait there for the slaughter.

Þorleifr also thought the people he had met were unfortunate because all of them were, in his opinion, completely defenceless, helpless, and unadapted to life. Nobody now knew how to use weapons, or even carried them, and consequently nobody could protect himself and his dependents from anyone who took it into his head to kill, rob, or rape them. Nobody knew how to do everything that a man must do in order to provide for himself and his household. A man now usually knew how to do only one thing, and often, it seemed, something completely unnecessary – like sitting at a desk and writing documents, the only purpose of which was to make it necessary to write still more documents; or sitting at a desk, pretending to be busy with something important and forcing others to wait until one stops pretending to be busy with something important; or sitting and listening to idle talk and from time to time raising one's hand to express a desire to take part in this idle talk. Þorleifr recalled here, though, that even in his own day the first settlers of Iceland had been held up as examples to his contemporaries – Skalla-Grímr Kveldúlfsson, for example, about whom it is reported, in *Egils saga*, that he could increase his livestock, build ships, sail and fish, and at the same time he played ball skilfully, and was a clever smith, an excellent fighter, and a good skald. Þorleifr thought that in our day people themselves understand their own defencelessness, helplessness and lack of adaptation to life, i. e. their doom. As a symbol of this doom, he supposed, they usually wear a noose around their necks (he evidently meant our neckties).

Our modern attire puzzled Þorleifr generally. Only as voluntary martyrdom, he thought, could we wear something as uncomfortable and ugly as, for example, our jackets. It also seemed voluntary martyrdom to him that people in our day do not ride on horseback as in his time, but ride in some sort of iron coffins which are not only ugly, but also unbearably noisy and unbearably smelly. Indeed, these iron coffins are inferior to horses not only in looks – here Þorleifr recalled with feeling the clever bay beauty he once loved to ride – but also in many other respects. For instance, they cannot find their own way, do not recognize their master, cannot secure their own food, and are no good at all for riding over mountains, lava fields, and sand. Moreover, Þorleifr marvelled, once accustomed to riding in the iron coffins, people forget how to walk – they can now walk only on paths as smooth and even as the floor in a house. Þorleifr evidently meant sidewalks.

Only one thing somewhat reconciled Þorleifr to the present – sagas, apparently, were still around. In any case, he had seen numerous books, as well as large sheets covered with small letters, and he supposed that all these were sagas.

Admittedly, he had not met a single good saga-teller. The only sagas he had heard in Reykjavík were very short, and were about only one thing – ghosts. Of course, in his time, too, Þorleifr admitted, it had happened that a corpse, especially if it had been a wicked man in life, climbed out of the grave, rode on the roof, killed livestock, attacked people, or did something that it had not succeeded in doing while alive. Þorleifr recalled several such cases. But, he marvelled, don't people really tell about any more important events now? Besides, the sagas Þorleifr had heard were, in his words, very poorly told – for instance, nothing was told in them of the ancestors of the people mentioned, and not everybody mentioned was even named.

As far as the large sheets covered with letters were

concerned, they did not interest Þorleifr in the least – they evidently contained such lying sagas that people as a rule discarded them as soon as they had read them, or simply used them as something easily crumpled and soft. Admittedly, it was incomprehensible to Þorleifr why these sagas were written, if they were so untruthful that they were not worth keeping.

On the other hand in our books, as Þorleifr thought, sagas are preserved which are worth reading, more than once. But he had managed to read only one of the books he had seen. He had selected it because, judging by its appearance, it was much read. Like all books that he had seen in present-day Iceland, it was written in very small letters, with which Þorleifr was completely unfamiliar, and there were many incomprehensible words in it, so that he mastered it only with great difficulty. On the very first page of this book was the account of a murder so base that, in Þorleifr's words, one could not read of it without revulsion. In his time, such murders did not happen. The murder was perpetrated at night, the blow was inflicted in the back, it was a blow from a poisoned weapon, and it was a woman who was killed, and an old and very respected woman at that. But still more striking, as it seemed to Þorleifr, was the fact that in the saga nothing was said of vengeance for this foul murder – and the murdered woman had many relatives, so that there was someone to carry out vengeance – but it was said only that it was impossible to guess who the killer was. If the narrator of this saga really did not know anything for certain, then why had be begun to tell the story? But, continued Þorleifr, he undoubtedly knew who the murderer was, because on the last page of the book it is told that the murderer was unmasked and confessed. The narrator, however, throughout the entire saga pretends that he does not know who the murderer is, and that he suspects, in turn, everybody mentioned in the saga (except the real murderer). He evidently tries in this way to please fools – they always like it when somebody else pretends to be a fool: they feel clever then.

Þorleifr was also struck by the fact that, although the narrator of the saga, in his words, lived "when this saga took place" (so Þorleifr expressed himself), he knows so little about the people mentioned in the saga, about their origins and the like, while at the same time he tells much that is completely superfluous – for example, in one place he says that the sun shone, the grass was green, and the hay smelled like hay. As if the sun could do anything else, or the grass could be any other color in the summertime, or hay not smell like hay. But Þorleifr was most amazed when he learned that everything told about in the saga he had read was simply invented for amusement. What ghoul, wondered Þorleifr, could think that such a foul murder was amusing? Besides, it was absolutely incomprehensible to him how it is possible to invent a saga taking place at the time the narrator is living. After all, it would be obvious to everybody also living at the time that the saga was a lie. Admittedly, confessed Þorleifr, in his day, too, there had been sagas telling of things which were difficult to believe, and such sagas had been considered amusing, although some people had called them lying sagas. But, continued Þorleifr, these sagas told of what happened in times immemorial and really no one could know exactly what had happened in times immemorial. Moreover, they say that things were possible then which are difficult to believe now – people were stronger and larger, and dragons and other monsters were still around.

It pained Þorleifr very much that the saga he had read, judging by the bedraggled condition of the book, was much read, and consequently, he concluded, was among the best of our sagas. What were the worst like, he asked, if this was one of the best? One had to confess that the saga he had read belonged to the most popular variety of sagas of our day, and at the same time one had to explain to him that the popularity of a saga, as a rule, has not, for a long time, stood in any sort of relation to its quality or to its truthfulness, and that therefore really true-to-life sagas, also set in modern times (admittedly, they were perhaps not "true" in the sense in which he used this word), are read by only a few. Yielding to Þorleifr's insistence, one had to tell him the contents of one of the famous works of this kind.

Þorleifr listened with great attention, but with still greater disbelief. He surmised that the gist of the saga had been left out. The tale was, actually, "about nothing", as he put it. Didn't the hero of the saga go on viking expeditions? Or perhaps he had some sort of feuds with other people? Could it be that in his entire life nothing happened, other than that he "made a fool of a certain woman" (Þorleifr expressed himself in this way about the romance forming the chief content of this work)? Or did perhaps some of this woman's relatives take vengeance on him, possibly not immediately, but after many years? Could it be that this "more-than-average-fool", as Þorleifr called the woman with whom the hero had his romance, was never able to incite any of the relatives to attack him? Or perhaps she had been abducted by force, and there was a battle? According to the puzzled Þorleifr, it was incomprehensible how a saga could be made of what had been told. If he were to retell it, he would simply say, "Everything was quiet", or "Nothing happened worth telling". One thing in the saga seemed to Þorleifr worthy of approval – in it there was, of course, no fiction.

But Þorleifr's puzzlement was boundless when he learned that, although the saga he had just heard is considered by all the cleverest people to be very true to life, nothing that is recounted in it actually ever took place, and that consequently the saga was, as Þorleifr concluded, simply a lie. It would have been understandable and pardonable, he reasoned, if the narrator had added some invention to the saga, supposedly occurring in remote times or in remote countries and increasing the glory of his ancestors or the ancestors of his friends. But to invent everything altogether, and there was nothing in the saga to tell about, anyway. What hardened liars people had become. Þorleifr was sadly surprised.

To try to convince Þorleifr that modern realistic literature is nonetheless, in a certain sense, truthful was obviously useless. Therefore, since he insistently asked to be told another famous saga, even a completely untruthful one, it seemed appropriate to tell him the contents of a modern work having a claim only to art, but not to realism. Þorleifr, listening, at first cheered up, the improbability of the story seemed to him so amusing – animals were supposed to be human beings, people to be gods, gods to be objects, and so on. Soon, however, he became serious, even sad. He was sorry, he explained, for the saga-teller – the latter had evidently lied so implausibly, not because he wanted to amuse, or even because he did not know how to lie plausibly (which is, of course, more difficult), but simply because he wanted to attract attention to himself – i. e., he was afraid of being unnoticed. In his own day, Þorleifr sorrowfully remarked, a saga-teller thought only of telling the saga well, and did not think of himself in the least. Þorleifr could not be convinced that (expressing his thought in modern terms) a rejection of realism cannot be explained merely by an inferiority complex of the author.

There was no point in continuing to try to acquaint Þorleifr with modern literature – it was obviously utterly incomprehensible to him. Since he insistently asked whether there were not, after all, in our day any really truthful sagas, there was nothing to do but tell him of our scholarly literature – in the first place, naturally, of literary history and criticism. But Þorleifr simply could not understand what either literary history and criticism, on the one hand, or a literary historian or critic, on the other, could be. Is the latter somebody who tells sagas about sagas? If he simply tells sagas which have already been told by somebody else, then how is he different from other saga-tellers? After all, any saga has already been told by somebody before, though perhaps in a different way – more expansively, more briefly, and so on. Or maybe, instead of telling a saga, he only says that he is going to tell it, but actually does not? Such a thing did happen to Þórir, Þorleifr's great-grandfather. Þórir was visiting a man named Ásgrímr (here Þorleifr recounted Ásgrímr's family tree). Instead of feeding Þórir, Ásgrímr only told him about food. Finally, Þórir killed Ásgrímr. Þorleifr was interested in knowing whether the same thing happens to those who tell sagas about sagas. Hearing that literary scholars do not tell sagas, but only say whether they are told well or poorly, Þorleifr was overjoyed – he thought he finally understood what a literary critic and historian is. There were also such people in his time, he said; they were, as he put it, the kind of silly fools who could tell absolutely nothing, but when others told some kind of story, constantly repeated, "Well told, very good!" But these silly fools were also sometimes nasty, in Þorleifr's words, and then upon hearing sagas, would constantly repeat, "Badly told, very bad!"

It seemed that the only possible way to give Þorleifr an idea of what literary scholarship and literary scholars are, was to tell him the contents of some concrete work of literary research. On the table in the room where this conversation was taking place a recently published work on one of the family sagas happened to be lying. From what is told in this saga it is concluded, among other things, that its hero often rode to the *alþingi* (like all Icelanders at that time), and that once when he was on the way there, it rained (as happens in Iceland very frequently). Manifesting dazzling erudition and a keen critical mind, the author of the work proved that a certain man, about whom absolutely nothing is known other than his name, the fact that he frequently rode to the *alþingi* and the fact that once when he was on his way there it rained, might have depicted himself as the hero of this family saga – in other words, he could be its author. The final proof that this man could indeed be the author of this saga turns out to be the fact that his name and the name of the hero begin with the same letter. By this agreement the author of the saga supposedly let it be known that he is depicting himself in the hero of the saga.

When Þorleifr heard which saga was meant, he pricked up his ears. It was clear that he knew quite well not only this saga itself, but also how it had been written. And when he heard what is being said about this saga in our day, he became still more sorrowful than before, and his eyes again filled with tears and he bitterly reproached the person who had disturbed him in his grave. And this is called truth! What a shameless liar one would have to be to give out as truth all the rubbish recounted in this "lying saga about a saga" (as Þorleifr called the work of literary scholarship just described to him). Þorleifr knew very well the man who was supposed to be the "author" (inventor, falsifier, liar? asked Þorleifr). This man had been completely truthful, and he never wrote sagas (Þorleifr indeed knew not only his name, but everything about him). The saga being discussed was not invented by anyone; it was the truth! Þorleifr knew this for certain, because he had written it himself . . .

It had already dawned, and the day was beginning.

Þorleifr's voice was barely audible, and his outlines had begun to melt in the air. And when he had completely disappeared, the author stood for a long time at the window and thought over what he had heard. It was on this morning that it occurred to him to write a book about the saga mind. And he then and there decided to end this book with a description of what he saw that morning from the window of his room on the sixth floor of the Saga Hotel. The square in front of the hotel was deserted. Reykjavík was still asleep. Slanting rays of the rising sun lit up the white walls and green and red roofs of the buildings. A strong westerly wind was blowing. One could see the waves breaking on the promontory beyond the city. Dark clouds were forming in the northwest. And to the north, beyond the fjord, the mountains were completely white. Evidently snow had fallen there during the night.

One can imagine what pity for modern humanity would have filled Þorleifr, if he had heard or read such an ending. A lyrical landscape, and at the end of a book claiming to be truthful to boot, would of course have seemed to him the summit of perversion and senselessness. What place do sunlit roofs, a rough sea, and newly fallen snow have here, he would have wondered. Þorleifr would have ended a saga simply by the ending. Unless, for complete clarity, he had added, "Here ends this saga."

Comments

> A scientific statement is a statement that can be disproved, by which we mean, of course, a statement worded in such a way as to make it clear what sort of data would be adequate to overthrow it.
>
> *Martin Joos*

Basic information concerning the family sagas is given below, along with a brief bibliography.

The family sagas tell of people and events of the first century after the settlement of Iceland – the period approximately from 930 to 1030. It is not known just how information concerning people and events of this preliterate age was preserved until the age when the family sagas were written down. These sagas are preserved chiefly in manuscripts of the fourteenth century or still later. All these manuscripts are copies from lost manuscripts. Only fragments of the family sagas are preserved from an earlier period, the earliest date from about the middle of the thirteenth century. It is considered certain that most of the family sagas were written during the course of the thirteenth century – the first at the beginning of the century, and the last at the beginning of the fourteenth century or later. A great deal, however, remains questionable in the dating of the family sagas, and not a single one of them can be dated with any degree of certainty. Their origin is also questionable, although recently most scholars have favoured the theory that they do not represent a written form of oral tradition, but are written works created by their authors.

The term "sagas of Icelanders" (Icelandic *Íslendinga sögur*, Norwegian *Islendingesagaer*, German *Isländersagas*) has recently become the most usual. But, as is proper for a scholarly term, it is actually meaningless – these sagas are not just any sagas telling of Icelanders, and they do not only include sagas in the true meaning of the word. Sagas about Icelanders living after the eleventh century do not belong with them. One of these latter sagas is even called *Íslendinga saga* (it was written by Sturla Þórðarson and forms part of *Sturlunga saga*). But this *Íslendinga saga* is not a "saga of Icelanders" or family saga. Sagas of Icelandic bishops also do not belong here. On the other hand, short accounts of Icelanders forming fragments (*þættir*, literally "strands") of the kings' sagas are usually assigned to the "sagas of Icelanders" or family sagas. Formerly the term "family sagas" (German *Familiensagas*, Norwegian *ættesagaer*) was the most frequently used. [It is used throughout this translation for convenience and consistency.] Many of these sagas are indeed histories of families. But this term became unpopular because it is linked with an unpopular idea of their origin ("family sagas" supposedly signifies folklore tradition rather than literary works). These sagas are also called simply "Icelandic sagas", since they are the most distinctive and the most famous of the Old Icelandic sagas. But the term "Icelandic sagas" is actually tautological, since, although some sagas of Norwegian origin are known and the word *saga* itself is common Scandinavian, sagas are chiefly an Icelandic genre. Therefore these sagas are frequently called simply "sagas". The word "saga" in the title of this book, for example, is used in this sense.

In all, about forty family sagas have been preserved (not counting the so-called *Íslendinga þættir* preserved in the kings' sagas). In Old Icelandic literature there are references to lost family sagas. But the authors of the family sagas are not mentioned anywhere in Old Icelandic literature, and attempts to identify them have not led to any sort of convincing results. Recently, the following sagas have usually been counted among the earliest (1200–1230): *Heiðarvíga saga, Hallfreðar saga, Kormáks saga, Fóstbræðra saga, Egils saga, Bjarnar saga.* To the period 1230–1280 are usually assigned *Víga-Glúms saga, Reykdœla saga, Ljósvetninga saga, Valla-Ljóts saga, Droplaugarsona saga, Vápnfirðinga saga, Gísla saga, Eyrbyggja saga,* and *Vatnsdœla saga.* Among the later ones are *Bandamanna saga, Gunnlaugs saga, Hœnsa-Þóris saga, Hrafnkels saga Freysgoða,* and *Njáls saga.* Still later are *Grettis saga, Harðar saga, Þórðar saga hreðu, Gull-Þóris saga, Svarfdœla saga, Hávarðar saga, Fljótsdœla saga,* and *Flóamanna saga.* Among the last written (not earlier than the fourteenth century) belong *Kjalnesinga saga, Víglundar saga, Bárðar saga Snæfellsáss, Króka-Refs saga,* and *Finnboga saga.* These latest family sagas are less original than the rest – in them there is much that is stereotyped and fantastic or romantic, and they are therefore usually not considered genuine family sagas. There are also family sagas written only in the nineteenth century, but these are simply imitations.

Each family saga is linked with a certain locality in Iceland, and in surveys these sagas are customarily arranged not in chronological order (this is too unclear), but in, as it were, geographical order. The following are connected with localities on the west coast of Iceland: *Harðar saga, Egils saga, Bjarnar saga, Gunnlaugs saga, Hœnsa-Þóris saga, Eyrbyggja saga, Laxdœla saga, Gísla saga, Fóstbræðra saga, Hávarðar saga.* These are connected with localities in the north: *Bandamanna saga, Kormáks saga, Grettis saga, Heiðarvíga saga, Vatnsdœla saga, Hallfreðar saga, Svarfdœla saga, Valla-Ljóts saga, Víga-Glúms saga, Ljósvetninga saga, Reykdœla saga.* These with the east: *Droplaugarsona saga, Vápnfirðinga saga, Fljótsdœla saga, Hrafnkels saga,* and several other short sagas. Only *Njáls saga* and *Flóamanna saga* are linked with southern districts.

Eiríks saga rauða and *Grœnlendinga saga* tell of Icelanders in North America and Greenland. The longest family sagas are *Njáls saga, Egils saga, Grettis saga, Laxdœla saga,* and *Eyrbyggja saga.* Several of the others are quite short. In many of the family sagas skaldic verses are cited. They appear most frequently in *Kormáks saga, Grettis saga, Egils saga,* and *Fóstbrœðra saga.* There are none at all in most of the sagas of the eastern region.

There are bibliographies of the family sagas in several volumes of the series *Islandica*; see Halldór Hermannsson, *Bibliography of the Icelandic Sagas (Islandica,* I, Ithaca, 1908), and *The Sagas of Icelanders* (*Islandica,* XXIV, Ithaca, 1935); and Jóhann S. Hannesson, *The Sagas of Icelanders (Islandica,* XXXVIII, Ithaca, 1957).

The best edition of the family sagas is the series *Íslenzk fornrit* (Reykjavík, 1933-). Each volume contains an extensive introduction and commentary. A popular Icelandic edition is *Íslendinga sögur,* Guðni Jónsson bjó til prentunar (Reykjavík: Íslendingasagnaútgáfan, 1953), I–XIII. A German edition, which includes other sagas than family sagas and has excellent commentaries, is *Altnordische Saga-Bibliothek* I–XVIII (Halle, 1892–1929). There are also numerous editions of individual family sagas.

Most of the family sagas have not been translated into Russian. Only the following have been translated: *Gunnlaugs saga, Egils saga, Laxdœla saga,* and *Njáls saga,* all four in the book *Islandskie sagi* (Leningrad, 1956); *Eiríks saga rauða* translated by S. N. Syromjatnikov (St Petersburg, 1890); and *Finnboga saga* translated by F. D. Batjuškov in the *Žurnal Ministerstva Narodnogo Prosveščenija,* 1885, Feb., 217–277, and July, 53–109. The last two translations were reprinted in *Drevnesevernye sagi i pesni skal'dov,* in the series *Russkaja klassnaja biblioteka,* ed. A. N. Čudinov, Series 2, No. 25 (St Petersburg, 1903). *Gunnlaugs saga* was earlier translated by E. N. Ščepkin in *Letopis' Istoriko-filo-*

logičeskogo obščestva pri Novorossijskom universitete, XII (1905), supplements, 87–140. An abridged translation of *Grettis saga* appeared in O. Peterson and E. Balabanova, *Zapadno-evropejskij èpos i srednevekovyj roman v pereskazax i sokraščennyx perevodax,* II (St Petersburg, 1896). In this book there is also a paraphrase of *Gunnlaugs saga.*

There are numerous translations of the family sagas in German, English, Norwegian, Swedish, and Danish.

The literature on family sagas is vast. General works, including literary histories, are given below: K. Schier, *Sagaliteratur* (Stuttgart, 1970; general information and bibliography). J. de Vries, *Altnordische Literaturgeschichte,* II (2nd ed., Berlin, 1967). T. M. Andersson, *The Icelandic Family Saga: an Analytic Reading* (Cambridge, Mass., 1967; with synopses of all the sagas and literature on the individual sagas). O. Widding, "Islændingesagaer", in *Norrøn fortællekunst* (Copenhagen, 1965), 72–91 and 156–162. P. G. Foote,"Some Account of the Present State of Saga Research", *Scandinavica,* IV (1965), 115–126. Einar Ólafur Sveinsson, "Islendingasögur", in *Kulturhistoriskt lexikon för nordisk medeltid,* VII (Malmö, 1962), cols. 496–513. Stefán Einarsson, *A History of Icelandic Literature* (New York, 1957). F. Paasche, *Norges og Islands litteratur inntil utgangen av middelalderen* (2nd ed., Oslo, 1957). P. Hallberg, *Den isländska sagan* (Stockholm, 1956); there are English, German and Danish translations. G. Turville-Petre, *Origins of Icelandic Literature* (Oxford, 1953). S. Nordal, "Sagalitteraturen", in *Nordisk Kultur* (Stockholm-Oslo-Copenhagen, 1953), VIII B, 180–273 (an interesting attempt to arrange all the sagas in order of their writing). H. E. Kinck, *Sagaenes ånd og skikkelser* (Oslo, 1951; much that is original concerning the saga characters). H. Laxness, "Minnisgreinar um fornsögur", *Tímarit máls og menningar,* 1945, 13–56; also in his books *Sjálfsagðir hlutir* (Reykjavík, 1946) and *De islandske sagaer og andre essays* (Copenhagen, 1963). A. Heusler, *Die altgermanische Dichtung* (2nd ed., Postdam, 1941; the chapter on the sagas is the best of the short essays). B. M. Ólsen, "Um Íslendingasögur, kaflar úr Háskólafyrirlestrum", *Safn til sögu Íslands og íslenzkra bókmennta að fornu og nýju,* VI (1937–1939), 1–428. Jón Helgason, *Norrøn Litteraturhistorie* (Copenhagen, 1934). H. Koht, *The Old Norse Sagas* (New York, 1931). B. Phillpotts, *Edda and Saga* (London, 1931). Finnur Jónsson, *Den oldnorske og oldislandske litteraturs historie,* II–III (2nd ed., Copenhagen, 1923–1924; a very detailed survey of all the family sagas). W. S. Craigie, *The Icelandic Sagas* (Cambridge, 1913). G. Neckel, "Von der isländischen Saga", *Germanisch-romanische Monatsschrift,* III (1911), 369–381 and 439–452. W. P. Ker, *Epic and Romance,* (2nd ed., London, 1908). A. Bonus, *Isländerbuch,* III (Munich, 1907). A. Olrik, *Nordisk Aandsliv i Vikingetid og tidlig Middelalder* (Copenhagen, 1907); there are German and English translations. E. Mogk, *Geschichte der norwegisch-isländischen Literatur* (2nd ed, Strassburg, 1904). R. Heinzel, "Beschreibung der isländischen Saga", *Sitzungsberichte der Kaiserlichen Akademie der Wissenschaften,* phil.-hist. Cl., XCVII (Vienna, 1881), 107–308. G. Vigfusson, "Prolegomena", in *Sturlunga Saga,* ed. G. Vigfusson, I (Oxford, 1878), xvi-ccxiv (a survey of Old Icelandic litterature, including all the family sagas). B. Döring, "Bemerkungen über Stil und Typus der isländischen Saga", in *Programm des Nicolaigymnasiums in Leipzig* (Leipzig, 1877), 1–44. C. Hauch, "Indledning til Forelæsninger over Njalssaga og flere med den beslægtede Sagaer", in his book *Afhandlinger og æsthetiske Betragtninger* (Copenhagen, 1855), 411–467 (the first attempt at treatment of the family saga as a variety of the novel). T. Möbius, *Über die ältere isländische Saga* (Leipzig, 1852). P. E. Müller, *Sagabibliothek med Anmærkninger,* I (Copenhagen, 1817).

In Russian: M. I. Steblin-Kamenskij, *Kul'tura Islandii* (Leningrad, 1967), 120–149; "O realizme islandskix sag", *Vestnik LGU*, Ser. istorii, jazyka i literatury (1965), No. 8, 2, 107–115; "Islandskaja rodovaja saga", *Romano-germanskaja filologija: Sb. statej v čest' V. F. Šišmareva* (Leningrad, 1957), 281–290; see also the introduction to *Islandskie sagi* (Leningrad, 1956), 1–19.

There are also many publications concerning the individual sagas, especially *Njáls saga, Egils saga*, and *Laxdœla saga* (see n. 29, p. 168), as well as the various aspects of the study of the family sagas (many of these works are cited in the notes below).

Notes to chapters 1–7

NB

1. An interesting attempt to discover how the meanings of words in an ancient language differ from the corresponding words in a modern language is presented in E. Leisi, "Aufschlußreiche altenglische Wortinhalte", in *Sprache, Schlüssel zur Welt: Festschrift für L. Weisgerber* (Düsseldorf, 1959), 309–318.
2. The philological investigation alluded to is devoted to the first husband of the wife of the famous collector of Icelandic manuscripts, Árni Magnússon. See Chr. Westergård-Nielsen, *Hvem var Arne Magnussons Formand?,* Institut for vestnordisk, Småskrifter, 1 (Århus, 1966).
3. Attempts at a structural analysis of the family sagas are to be found in the following: G. Hellwig, *Die Struktur der Hallfreðar Saga* (Munich, 1967). H. M. Heinrichs, "Die künstlerische Gestaltung des Þorsteins þáttr stangarhöggs", in *Festschrift W. Baetke* (Weimar, 1966), 167–174. A. C. Bouman, *Patterns in Old English and Old Icelandic Literature* (Leiden, 1962). M. C. van den Toorn, "Zur Struktur der Saga", *Arkiv för nordisk filologi,* LXXIII (1958), 140–168.
4. Truth and fiction in the family sagas are, as a rule, treated in all the works concerning these sagas. But there are also works devoted especially to this problem. See M. I. Steblin-Kamensky, "On the Nature of Fiction in the Sagas of Icelanders", *Scandinavica,* VI (1967), 77–84; H. Magerøy, "Dikt og sanning i islendingesogene", *Syn og Segn,* LXIV (1958), 145–152; M. C. van den Toorn, "Saga und Wirklichkeit", *Arkiv för nordisk filologi,* LXXII (1957), 193–205; S. Nordal, *The Historical Element in the Icelandic Family Sagas* (Glasgow, 1957);

G. Jones, "History and Fiction in the Sagas of the Icelanders", *Saga-Book of the Viking Society,* XIII (1952–1953), 285–306; E. Jessen, "Glaubwürdigkeit der Egils-Saga und anderer Isländer-Saga's", *Historische Zeitschrift,* XXVIII (1872), 61–100.

5. On the meanings of the Old Icelandic words examined here see also M. E. Steblin-Kamenskij, "An Attempt at a Semantic Approach to the Problem of Authorship in Old Icelandic Literature", *Arkiv för nordisk filologi,* LXXXI (1966), 24–34; L. Lönnroth, *European Sources of Icelandic Saga-Writing* (Stockholm, 1965), 6 ff.
6. The theory that the courtly romance was the prototype of the family sagas was launched by the Danish critic P. V. Rubow in "De islandske sagaer", *Tilskueren* (1928), I, 347–357; II, 170–174; and also in the book *Smaa kritiske Breve* (Copenhagen, 1936), 7–33. Rubow's article, very naive as literary history, nevertheless exercised great influence on Icelandic scholars.
7. Much has been written on the famous utterance at the feast at Reykjahólar in 1119. One of the most recent essays on it is P. G. Foote, "Sagnaskemtan: Reykjahólar 1119", *Saga-Book of the Viking Society,* XIV (1955–1956), 226–239. See also U. Brown, "The Saga of Hrómund Gripsson and Þorgils Saga", *Saga-Book of the Viking Society,* XIII (1947–1948), 51–77; and her *Þorgils saga ok Hafliða* (Oxford and London, 1952).
8. How Snorri paraphrased his sources is well demonstrated in H. Lie, *Studier i Heimskringlas stil: dialogene og talene,* Skrifter utgitt av det Norske Videnskaps-Akademi i Oslo, II. kl., 1936, no. 5 (Oslo, 1937).
9. On dreams in the family sagas, see G. Turville-Petre, "Dream Symbols in Old Icelandic Literature", in *Festschrift W. Baetke* (Weimar, 1966), 334–354; G. D. Kelchner, *Dreams in Old Norse Literature and their Affinities in Folklore* (Cambridge, 1935); M. Haeckel, *Die Darstellung und Funktion des Traumes in der isländischen Familiensaga* (Hamburg, 1934); W. Henzen, *Über die Träume in der altnordischen Sagalitteratur* (Leipzig, 1890).

10. On saga genres, see L. Lönnroth, *European Sources of Icelandic Saga-Writing* (Stockholm, 1965), 6–11.
11. *Sturlunga saga* covers the period 1117–1266, and was apparently written in the thirteenth century. The most recent edition is *Sturlunga saga,* Jón Jóhannesson, Magnús Finnbogason og Kristján Eldjárn sáu um útgáfuna, I–II (Reykjavík, 1946), with an extensive introduction and detailed commentary. Several of the sagas making up *Sturlunga saga* have also been published separately.
12. The most consistent treatment of the family sagas as *romans à clef* will be found in Barði Guðmundsson, *Höfundur Njálu* (Reykjavík, 1958); this is a posthumous edition of his articles.
13. On epic stylization in the family sagas, see e. g. H. Dehmer, *Primitives Erzählungsgut in den Íslendinga-Sögur* (Leipzig, 1927); L. A. Bock, "Die epische Dreizahl in den Íslendinga sǫgur", *Arkiv för nordisk filologi,* XXXVII (1920), 263–313; XXXVIII (1921), 51–83.
14. On the sagas of olden times (*fornaldarsögur*), in addition to the literary histories and general works on the sagas cited above, see Einar Ól. Sveinsson, "Fornaldarsögur Norðurlanda", in *Kulturhistoriskt lexikon för nordisk medeltid,* IV (Malmö, 1959), cols. 499–507; M. Schlauch, *Romance in Iceland* (Princeton, 1934); H. Reuschel, *Untersuchungen über Stoff und Stil der Fornaldarsaga* (Leipzig, 1933). For bibliographies of these sagas, see Halldór Hermannsson, *Bibliography of the Mythical-Heroic Sagas* (*Islandica,* V, Ithaca, 1912); *The Sagas of the Kings and the Mythical-Heroic Sagas: Two Bibliographical Supplements* (*Islandica,* XXVI, Ithaca, 1937). These sagas were so named by their first editor, C. C. Rafn, in *Fornaldar Sögur Norðrlanda,* I–III (Copenhagen, 1829–1830). They have most recently been published by Guðni Jónsson in three vols. (Reykjavík: Íslendingasagnaútgáfan, 1950). There are also numerous editions of individual sagas of olden times. There is, however, no clearcut dividing line between these sagas and medieval Icelandic romances. For an edition of the latter, see *Late Medieval Icelandic Romances,* ed. A. Loth, I–V

(Copenhagen, 1962–1965). Only the following have been translated into Russian: *Friðþjófs saga,* translated by Ja. K. Grot (2nd ed., Voronež, 1874) and by A. I. Smirnickij (published by "Academia" in 1935); *Vǫlsunga saga,* translated by B. I. Jarxo (published by "Academia" in 1934); excerpts from *Ǫrvar-Odds saga* and several other sagas, cited in K. F. Tiander, *Poezdki skandinavov v Beloe more* (St Petersburg, 1906); fragments of *Hervarar saga* are given in I. Šarovol'skij, *Skazanie o meče Tjurfinge,* I and III (Kiev, 1906).

15. On kings' sagas, see, in addition to the literary histories and general works on the sagas cited above, the following: A. Holtsmark, "Kongesaga", in *Kulturhistoriskt lexikon för nordisk medeltid,* IX (Malmö, 1961), cols. 41–46; S. Beyschlag, *Konungasögur* (Copenhagen, 1950); Bjarni Aðalbjarnarson, *Om de norske kongers sagaer,* Skrifter utgitt av Det Norske Videnskaps-Akademi i Oslo, II. kl., 1936, no. 4 (Oslo, 1937); T. Berntsen, *Fra sagn til saga: Studier i kongesagaen* (Christiania, 1923); G. A. Gjessing, *Undersøgelse af Kongesagaens Fremvæxt,* I–II (Christiania, 1873–1876). For bibliographies of these sagas, see Halldór Hermannsson, *Bibliography of the Sagas of the Kings of Norway and Related Sagas and Tales* (*Islandica,* III, Ithaca, 1919); *The Sagas of the Kings . . .* (*Islandica,* XXVI, Ithaca, 1937). The separate kings' sagas have been published many times, but a critical collected edition is still wanting. The best edition of Snorri Sturluson's *Heimskringla,* the most famous of them, is in *Íslenzk fornrit,* XXVI–XXVIII (Reykjavík, 1941–1951), with an extensive introduction by Bjarni Aðalbjarnarson. In Russian translation there are only *Eymundar saga,* translated by O. I. Senkovskij in *Biblioteka dlja čtenija,* II (1834), 1–71; reprinted in his *Sobranie sočinenij* [*Collected Works*] (St Petersburg, 1858), V, 511–573; and part of *Óláfs saga Tryggvasonar,* translated by S. Sabinin in *Russkij istoričeskij sbornik, izdavaemyj Obščestvom istorii i drevnostej rossijskix,* IV (1840), iii–v and 7–116. These translations were reprinted in *Drevnesevernye sagi i pesni skal'dov,* in the series *Russkaja*

klassnaja biblioteka, ed. A. N. Čudinov, Series 2, No. 25 (St Petersburg, 1903).

16. The bishops' sagas embrace the period from approximately 1000 to 1340, and were written from about 1200 to 1350. See Magnús M. Lárusson, "Biskupa sögur", in *Kulturhistoriskt lexikon för nordisk medeltid,* I (Malmö, 1956), cols. 630–631. For the edition of the bishops' sagas, see *Biskupa sögur,* gefnar út af hinu íslenzka bókmentafélagi, I–II (Copenhagen, 1858–1878). This edition was reprinted in the popular Icelandic edition *Biskupa sögur,* Íslendingasagnaútgáfan, I–III (Reykjavík, 1948). In 1938 Jón Helgason began a new edition of the bishops' sagas.
17. Statistical methods to determine the authors of the sagas have been employed by the Swedish literary scholar Peter Hallberg in many publications; see e. g. *Stilsignalement och författarskap i norrön sagalitteratur* (Göteborg, 1968); "Om språkliga författarkriterier i isländska sagatexter", *Arkiv för nordisk filologi,* LXXX (1965), 157–186. Lönnroth has criticized the method, see e. g. *Samlaren,* LXXXIV (1963), 280–285.
18. For work on the meanings of the words analyzed, see n. 5.
19. There is a very large quantity of literature on the origin of the family sagas. The most recent surveys of the problem are T. M. Andersson, *The Problem of Icelandic Saga Origins: a Historical Survey* (New Haven and London, 1964); and M. Scovazzi, *La saga di Hrafnkell e il problema delle saghe islandesi* (Brescia, 1960). The viewpoint prevalent in the first half of the nineteenth century is represented in the following publications: P. E. Müller, *Über den Ursprung und Verfall der isländischen Historiographie* (Copenhagen, 1813); *Sagabibliothek med Anmærkninger,* I (Copenhagen, 1817); R. Keyser, "Nordmændenes Videnskabelighed og Litteratur i Middelalderen", in *Efterladte Skrifter,* I (Christiania, 1886). A turn in the direction of the "book-prose theory" began to show itself in K. Maurer, "Die norwegische Auffassung der nordischen Literatur-Geschichte", *Zeitschrift für deutsche Philologie,* I (1869), 25–28. The "free-prose theory" is represented in the following: R.

Meissner, *Die Strengleikar: ein Beitrag zur Geschichte der altnordischen Prosaliteratur* (Halle, 1902); G. Neckel, "Von der isländischen Saga", *Germanisch-romanische Monatsschrift,* III (1911), 369–381 and 439–452; A. Heusler, *Die Anfänge der isländischen Saga,* Abhandlungen der Preuss. Akademie d. Wiss., phil.-hist. Cl., 1913, 9 (Berlin, 1914), also in *Kleine Schriften,* 2nd ed., II (Berlin, 1969), 388–460; E. Olson, "Den isländska sagans ursprung", *Nordisk tidskrift för vetenskap, konst och industri,* 1918, 411–429; K. Liestøl, *Upphavet til den islendske ættesoga* (Oslo, 1929) (English translation: *The Origin of the Icelandic Family Sagas* [Oslo, 1930]); idem, "Tradisjon og forfattar i den islendske ættesoga", *Maal og minne,* 1936, 1–16. The "book-prose theory", revived by Icelandic scholars, is represented in e. g. the following: B. M. Ólsen, "Um Íslendingasögur", *Safn til sögu Íslands og íslenzkra bókmennta að fornu og nýju,* VI (1937–1939), 1–428; S. Nordal, *Snorri Sturluson* (Reykjavík, 1920); idem, introduction to *Egils saga Skallagrímssonar* (*Íslenzk fornrit,* II, Reykjavík, 1933), v–vc; idem, *Hrafnkatla* (*Studia Islandica,* VII, Reykjavík, 1940); idem, "Sagalitteraturen", in *Nordisk Kultur,* VIII B (Stockholm-Oslo-Copenhagen, 1953), 180–273; Einar Ól. Sveinsson, "The Icelandic Sagas and the period in which they were written", *Acta Philologica Scandinavica,* XII (1937–1938), 71–90; idem, *Á Njálsbúð* (Reykjavík, 1943); idem, introduction to *Brennu-Njáls saga* (*Íslenzk fornrit,* XII, Reykjavík, 1954), v–clxiii. A sharp criticism of the methods of the Icelandic school may be found in H. Lie, "Noen metodologiske overveielser i anl. av et bind av *Íslenzk fornrit*", *Maal og minne,* 1939, 97–138. A complete negation of the historical element and of the role of oral tradition in the family sagas is found in W. Baetke, *Über die Entstehung der Isländersagas,* Berichte über die Verhandlungen der Sächs. Akademie der Wiss. zu Leipzig, phil.-hist. Kl., 102, 5 (Berlin, 1956). A sharp criticism of this work is found in a review by H. Kuhn in *Anzeiger für deutsches Altertum und deutsche Literatur,* LXXV (1964), 73–75. A compromise viewpoint as far as family sagas are concerned is represented in e. g. D. Strömbäck, "Von der isländischen Familiensaga", *Beiträge zur Geschichte der deutschen Sprache und Literatur* (Halle, 1942), 117–133; J. de Vries, "Die isländische Saga und die mündliche Überlieferung", in *Märchen, Mythos, Dichtung: Festschrift für F. von der Leyen* (Munich, 1965), 169–176.

20. On methods of dating the family sagas, see Einar Ól. Sveinsson, *Dating the Icelandic Sagas: an Essay in Method* (London, 1958); in Icelandic (revised) *Ritunartími Íslendingasagna, rök og rannsóknaraðferð* (Reykjavík, 1965).
21. On characterization in the family sagas, see A. Hruby, *Zur Technik der isländischen Saga: die Kategorien ihrer Personencharakteristik* (Vienna, 1929).
22. On the specific character of proper names in Old Icelandic literature, see M. I. Steblin-Kamenskij, "Drevneislandskaja toponomastika kak material k istorii imeni sobstvennogo", *Skandinavskij sbornik,* XIV (1969), 99–105.
23. For discussion of the style of the family sagas, see O. Springer, "The Style of the Old Icelandic Family Sagas", *Journal of English and Germanic Philology,* XXXVIII (1934), 107–128. On dialogue in the family sagas, see I. Netter, *Die direkte Rede in den Isländersagas* (Leipzig, 1935); W. Ludwig, *Untersuchungen über den Entwicklungsgang und die Funktion des Dialogs in der isländischen Saga* (Halle, 1934); M. Jeffrey, *The Discourse in Seven Icelandic Sagas: Droplaugarsona saga, Hrafnkels saga Freysgoða, Víga-Glúms saga, Gísla saga, Fóstbræðra saga, Hávarðar saga, Flóamanna saga* (Menasha, 1934). On simile in the family sagas, see P. Schach, "The Use of the Simile in the Old Icelandic Family Sagas", *Scandinavian Studies,* XXIV (1952), 149–156. On metaphor, see M. Müller, *Verhüllende Metaphorik in der Saga: ein Beitrag zur Kulturpsychologie Altislands* (Würzburg-Aumühle, 1939). On word order in the family sagas, see G. S. Rieger, "Die Spitzen-Stellung des finiten Verbs als Stilmittel des isländischen Sagaerzählers", *Arkiv för nordisk filologi,* LXXXIII (1968), 81–139. On reference to oral tradition in the family sagas, see T. M. Andersson, "The textual evidence for an oral Family

Saga", *Arkiv för nordisk filologi,* LXXXI (1966), 1–23. On style in individual sagas, see A. C. Bouman, *Observations on Syntax and Style of some Icelandic Sagas with special Reference to the Relation between Víga-Glúms saga and Reykdœla saga* (*Studia Íslandica,* XVa, Reykjavík, 1956), which consists chiefly of statistical tabulations.

24. On skaldic *vísur* in the family sagas see A. Wolf, "Zur Rolle der *vísur* in der altnordischen Prosa", in *Festschrift L. C. Franz* (Innsbruck, 1965), 459–484; Bjarni Einarsson, *Skáldasögur: um uppruna og eðli ástaskáldasagnanna fornu* (Reykjavík, 1961); A. Hruby, *Wann sprechen die Personen der isländischen Saga eine Strophe? Eine Studie zur Technik der Saga* (Vienna, 1932); Finnur Jónsson, "Sagaernes lausavísur", in *Aarbøger for nordisk Oldkyndighed,* 1912, 1–57. There is much literature devoted to the interpretation of *vísur* in individual sagas. Regarding skaldic poetry in general, see M. I. Steblin-Kamenskij, *Kul'tura Islandii* (Leningrad, 1967), 88–119 and 177–178.
25. On *Íslendinga þættir* as a literary form see W. Lange, "Einige Bemerkungen zur altnordischen Novelle", *Zeitschrift für deutsches Altertum und deutsche Literatur,* LXXXVIII (1957), 150–159.
26. On different treatments of the same or similar events in different family sagas, see A. Heusler, "Berührungen zwischen den Isländergeschichten", in *Kleine Schriften,* 2nd ed., II (Berlin, 1969), 321–346.
27. On types in the family sagas, see R. Heller, *Die literarische Darstellung der Frau in den Isländersagas* (*Saga,* II; Halle/Saale, 1958); W. Emmerich, *Untersuchungen zur Rolle von Intriganten und Bösewichten in einigen Íslendinga sǫgur* (Leipzig, 1955).
28. On the depiction of emotions in the family sagas, see Sveinn Bergsveinsson, "Sagaen og den haardkogte roman", *Edda,* XLII (1942), 56–62; H. Kinck, *Sagaenes ånd og skikkelser* (Oslo, 1951); H. J. Graf, *Untersuchungen zur Gebärde in der Íslendingasaga* (Lengerich, 1938); A. Gödecke, *Die Darstellung der Gemütsbewegungen in der isländischen Familiensaga* (Hamburg, 1933).

29. There are many publications concerning *Laxdœla saga.* A list of them can give an idea of how the individual family sagas are studied: R. Heller, "Der Verfasser der Laxdœla saga und sein Verhältnis zur Sturlubók", in *Afmælisrit Jóns Helgasonar* (Reykjavík, 1969), 80–91; idem, "Das Alter der Laxdœla saga", *Zeitschrift für deutsches Altertum und deutsche Literatur,* XCVII (1968), 134–155; idem, "Neue Wege zur Verfasserbestimmung bei den Isländersagas und ihre Anwendung auf die Laxdœla saga", *Forschungen und Fortschritte,* XLI (1967), 239–242; idem, "Gísla saga Súrssonar und Laxdœla saga", in *Festschrift W. Baetke* (Weimar, 1966), 181–190; idem, "Droplaugarsona saga – Vápnfirðinga saga – Laxdœla saga", *Arkiv för nordisk filologi,* LXXVIII (1963), 140–169; idem, "Laxdœla saga und Bischofssagas", *Arkiv för nordisk filologi,* LXXVII (1962), 90–95; idem, *Laxdœla saga und Königssagas* (*Saga,* V; Halle, 1961); idem, "Laxdœla saga und Sturlunga saga", *Arkiv för nordisk filologi,* LXXVI (1961), 112–133; idem, *Literarisches Schaffen in der Laxdœla saga* (*Saga,* II; Halle, 1960); idem, "Studien zu Aufbau und Stil der Laxdœla saga", *Arkiv för nordisk filologi,* LXXV (1960), 113–167; M. Schildknecht-Burri, *Die altertümliche und jüngeren Merkmale der Laxdœla saga* (Lucerne, 1945); J. Drever, "The Psychology of Laxdœlasaga", *Saga-Book of the Viking Society,* XII (1937–45), 107–118; Einar Ól. Sveinsson, introduction to *Laxdœla saga* (*Íslenzk fornrit,* V, Reykjavík, 1934); A. C. Kersbergen, "Frásagnir in de Laxdœla saga", *Neophilologus,* XIX (1934), 53–68; J. van Ham, *Beschouwingen over de literaire betekenis der Laxdœla saga* (Amsterdam, 1932).
30. On ethical concepts in the family sagas, see M. C. van den Toorn, *Ethics and Moral in Icelandic Saga Literature* (Assen, 1955); Matthías Jónasson, "Die Grundnormen des Handelns bei den Isländern heidnischer Zeit", *Beiträge zur Geschichte der deutschen Sprache und Literatur,* LXVIII (1945–1946), 139–184; J. Hovstad, *Mannen og samfundet: studiar i norrøn etikk* (Oslo, 1943); H. Kuhn, "Sitte und Sittlichkeit", in *Germanische Altertumskunde* (Munich,

1938), 171–221; W. Gehl, *Ruhm und Ehre bei den Nordgermanen* (Berlin, 1937); A. Heusler, "Altgermanische
~~*Nordgermanen* (Berlin, 1937); A. Heusler, "Altgermanische~~
Sittenlehre und Lebensweisheit", in *Germanische Wiedererstehung* (Heidelberg, 1926), 156–204; V. Grønbech, *Vor Folkeæt i Oldtiden,* I–IV (Copenhagen, 1909–1912; English translation: *The Culture of the Teutons,* I–III [London, 1931]; German translation: *Kultur und Religion der Germanen* [Hamburg, 1937, Darmstadt, 1961]). See also the classic works on feuds in Iceland: A. Heusler, *Das Strafrecht der Isländersagas* (Leipzig, 1911); idem, "Zum isländischen Fehdewesen in der Sturlungazeit", *Abhandlungen der Preuss. Akad. der Wiss.,* phil.-hist. Cl., 1912, 1–102.

31. On the Sturlung age see R. G. Thomas, "The Sturlung Age as an Age of Saga Writing", *The Germanic Review,* XXV (1950), 50–66; Einar Ól. Sveinsson, *Sturlungaöld* (Reykjavík, 1940; English translation: *The Age of the Sturlungs* [London, 1953]); F. Paasche, *Snorre Sturlason og Sturlungerne* (Christiania, 1922; largely a retelling of *Sturlunga saga;* on this saga, see n. 11).
32. There are many publications which discuss paganism and Christianity in the family sagas. See e. g. L. Lönnroth, "The Noble Heathen: a Theme in the Sagas", *Scandinavian Studies,* XLI (1969), 1–29 (concerns the Christian reinterpretation of pagan heroes); M. Scovazzi, "Paganesimo e cristianesimo nelle saghe nordiche", in *Settimane di studio del centro italiano di studi sull'alto medioevo,* XIV (Spoleto, 1967), 759–794; W. Baetke, "Christliches Lehngut in der Sagareligion", *Berichte über die Verhandlungen der Sächs. Akademie der Wiss. zu Leipzig,* phil.-hist. Kl., XCVIII (1951), 7–55 (an interpretation of everything once considered pagan in the sagas as Christian); H. Kuhn, "Das nordgermanische Heidentum in den ersten christlichen Jahrhunderten", *Zeitschrift für deutsches Altertum und deutsche Literatur,* LXXIX (1942), 133–166 (concerns belief in pagan gods even after the Conversion); H. Ljungberg, *Den nordiska religionen och kristendomen: studier över det nordiska religionsskiftet under vikingatiden* (Uppsala, 1938);

B. Kummer, *Midgards Untergang: germanisches Kult und Glaube in den letzten heidnischen Jahrhunderten* (Leipzig, 1927; an idealization of paganism as a "Germanic religion" based chiefly on saga material); K. Maurer, *Die Bekehrung des norwegischen Stammes zum Christentum,* I–II (Munich, 1855–1856; an extremely rich collection of material).

33. On sorcery in the family sagas, see C. F. Bayerschmidt, "The Element of the Supernatural in the Sagas of Icelanders", in the H. G. Leach Festschrift, *Scandinavian Studies* (Seattle, 1965), 39–53; K. Jarausch, "Der Zauber in den Isländer-sagas", *Zeitschrift für Volkskunde,* I (1930), 237–268.
34. There is only one publication on conceptions of time in the family sagas – M. C. van den Toorn, "Zeit und Tempus in der Saga", *Arkiv för nordisk filologi,* LXXVI (1961), 134–152. But the problems treated in it are for the most part not touched on in the present book – e. g. the relation between "time of the narrative" and "narrated time", the tempo of the saga, and the role of grammatical tense. On grammatical tense in the family sagas see also P. M. Morris, *Das Futurum in den altisländischen Familiensagen: Ausdruck und Anwendung* (Munich, 1964); U. Sprenger, *Praesens historicum und Praeteritum in der altisländischen Saga: ein Beitrag zur Frage Freiprosa, Buchprosa* (Basel, 1951); W. Lehmann, *Das Präsens historicum in den Íslendinga sǫgur* (Würzburg-Aumühle, 1939). On chronology in all the family sagas, see Guðbrandur Vigfússon, "Um tímatal í Íslendinga sögum í fornöld", *Safn til sögu Íslands,* I (1855), 185–502. The content of this chapter in the present book essentially repeats the article by M. I. Steblin-Kamenskij, "Tidsforestillingene i islendingesagaene", *Edda,* LXVII (1968), 351–361.
35. On the belief in fate in the family sagas see G. Loescher, *Gestalt und Funktion der Vorausdeutung in der isländischen Saga-Literatur: Studien zur Interpretation der Isländersagas* (Tübingen, 1956; concerns prophecies as a compositional device); W. Wirth, *Der Schicksalsglaube in den Isländersagas* (Stuttgart-Berlin, 1940); W. Gehl, *Der germanische Schick-*

salsglaube (Berlin, 1939); A. U. Bååth, *Studier öfver kompositionen i några isländska ättsagor* (Lund, 1885; concerns belief in fate as a compositional device).

36. On the "living dead" in the family sagas, see H. J. Klare, "Die Toten in der altnordischen Literatur", *Acta Philologica Scandinavica,* VIII (1933–1934), 1–56; H. Neuberg, *Der Aberglaube in den Íslendinga sögur* (Riga, 1926).